when the train left the station

ossie *clark* 1965|74

Judith Watt

V&A Publications

First published by V&A Publications, 2003
V&A Publications
160 Brompton Road
London SW3 1HW

Text © Judith Watt 2003
Judith Watt asserts her moral right to be identified
as the author of this book

Designed by Vaughan Oliver at v23
Production by Studio 22
V&A photography by Pip Barnard and Sara Hodges,
V&A Photographic Studio

Archive material from the collection of Celia Birtwell
reproduced with her kind permission.

Front jacket: Photograph by Lichfield, Camera Press
London
Back jacket: Sketch by Celia Birtwell (see p.72)
Half-title page: Sketch by Ossie Clark, c. 1968–9
(see p. 80)
Frontispiece: Sketch by Celia Birtwell, c. 1969 (see p. 62)
Dedication page: Blouse, c. 1969 (see p. 90)

Printed in Italy

ISBN 1 85177 407 6

A catalogue record for this book is available
from the British Library.

V&A Publications
160 Brompton Road
London SW3 1HW
www.vam.ac.uk

Contents

for Celia

Foreword

Ossie Clark's most productive years coincided with London's most optimistic, rule-breaking period, when fashion, photography, music and the cult of personality converged. From 1965 to 1974 Ossie Clark dressed the famous and fashionable in unabashed show-stoppers. His eveningwear was boldly seductive; his tailoring deliciously precise; and above all, his clothes were feminine.

Born in Liverpool in 1942, Ossie Clark came to London to study fashion design at the Royal College of Art. When British *Vogue* singled him out in their August 1965 issue Ossie, at 23, emerged as a recognized new talent. *Vogue*'s continuing coverage documents what made him exceptional: facility with diverse materials, impressive cutting skills and an extraordinarily productive collaboration with his wife, the textile designer Celia Birtwell. Ossie's inventiveness and influence reinforced London's position as a leading fashion centre. He offered his clients a fresh alternative to the city's traditional couture houses and his designs for Alice Pollock's boutique, Quorum, helped make the King's Road a fashion destination.

Not only did Ossie Clark's clothes appeal to the elite but also, in an early example of mass-market appeal, his designs for the Radley label made London style available to thousands of ordinary people.

Ossie's glamorous life and tragic death in 1996 have overshadowed his importance as a highly skilled designer. The following pages remind us why Ossie mattered. Judith Watt has written a tribute to him that celebrates his talent and important contribution to recent fashion history.

The V&A, a source of inspiration for Ossie when he was a student and long a collector of his designs, is proud to present this volume.

Sonnet Stanfill
Curator of Contemporary Fashion
Department of Furniture, Textiles and Fashion

opposite
Ossie in his studio at Burnsall Street, wearing his trademark jumper hand-knit by his mother, c. 1970.

Introduction

'Fashion is about taking one out of reality, and this is what he achieved.' Manolo Blahnik

opposite
Ossie and Celia.
Vogue, *July 1970*.
**Annette Green © Vogue/
The Condé Nast Publications Ltd**

From the mid-1960s to mid-1970s, Ossie Clark was at the pinnacle of British fashion, with an international reputation as *the* London designer. Women loved to wear Ossie Clark. By the time of his death, however, he had suffered a series of emotional blows and financial setbacks, and the press appeared to be more fascinated by his *Rake's Progress*-style decline than the great talent that had once been.

His diaries, kept religiously from his time at the Royal College of Art, inspired by Mae West's dictum, 'Keep a diary and one day it will keep you,' were published posthumously in 1999. They could have been his best-known legacy had it not been for the exhibition 'Ossie Clark', held at Warrington Museum and Art Gallery in 1999–2000 and curated by Cherry Gray. [1] The exhibition was a revelation, its display of clothes from private collections a remarkable tribute both to his skills as a fashion designer and to the important collaboration

with his former wife, the textile designer Celia Birtwell. Sketchbooks, clothes, film footage and photographs revealed immense talent, energy and vision that reflected the mood of London in the period between the advent of Mary Quant's revolutionary mini-skirt and Malcolm McLaren and Vivienne Westwood's dystopian Punk. He was the first of the British 'young designers' to inhabit a celebrity world and to be one in his own right, but, more importantly, he was an innovator, whose influence went beyond the micro-culture of the King's Road. His experimentation with cutting, draping and fabric weight, from transparent chiffon to heavy wool, and his ability to work with a fabric designer, allowing her complete design freedom, produced an opus of work that is astonishing in variety. At the same time, he always kept in mind what it was for: a woman's body, and the more curvaceous and patently female the better. Mae West was, after all, one of his pin-ups. Such was

Ossie Clark dress,
print by Celia Birtwell, c. 1970.
Black chiffon with red tulip print.
Collection of Celia Birtwell

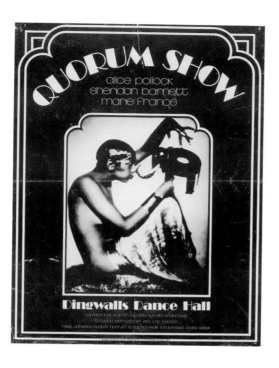

above left
Poster for the Quorum show at Dingwalls, 1973.

above right
Patti Boyd wearing a beige smock in crêpe with half sleeves above long voile cuffed sleeves, with an olive and orange print by Celia Birtwell, 14½ guineas, in 'Ossie Invents Summer, Patti Wears it'.
Vogue, *June 1969.*
David Bailey © Vogue/ The Condé Nast Publications Ltd

his appeal that the 'Ossie Clark for Quorum' collections were sold in both Europe and America and a diffusion line, 'Ossie Clark for Radley', sold in its thousands on the high street, making high fashion accessible for ordinary young women. 'Women feel special in my clothes,' he said, astutely. 'That's why I am successful.'

Ossie was a live wire: volatile, endearing, acerbic, difficult, brilliance packed into a small frame dressed in his mother's hand-knitted jumpers and a Celia print shirt or pistachio-green Tommy Nutter suit. As Marit Allen, his friend from her early days at *Vogue*, told me: he had personality. He loved nature: trees, flowers, the moon, stars, colour, natural form; all excited him, and his aim was to create beauty in his work, not to make enormous amounts of money, as is so often the yardstick by which a successful designer is measured today.

The word most often used by people who wore his clothes is 'magic', and they did have the power of transformation, what his Quorum colleague Fiona Ronaldson has revealingly called 'result-wear'. His brilliance lay in his ability to understand form and proportion and to achieve it through cut and fabric. Designers could draw 'until they are blue in the face, but that is not enough,' Ossie said in 1972. In a true sense, his inspiration came from designers of the past, Madeleine Vionnet and Charles James in particular, and the fashion illustrations in the *Gazette du Bon Ton*. Their creations he experienced first-hand at Victoria and Albert Museum through the teaching of Bernard Nevill while he was at the Royal College of Art. Although these were undoubtedly a starting-point for his work, it bore no taint of nostalgia. Up until 1974, his clothes were new and full of surprises.

*Quorum show, Spring 1970 at
Chelsea Town Hall. Amanda Lear,
at the front of the runway, wears a
silk chiffon wrap-around dress,
printed in charcoal grey and
pale pink. Janey Ironside is at the
far left with her arms raised.
It was at this show that one of the
models had to be dragged off the
stage because she wouldn't leave.
At Ossie shows, the runway
was a dance-floor and
models did it their way.*
Vogue, *July 1970.*
**Annette Green © Vogue/
The Condé Nast Publications Ltd**

His fashion shows were revolutionary theatrical events that contributed to his celebrity status, in venues as grand as the Albert Hall or as street-cred as Dingwalls in Camden Town. The seats were filled with the rich and famous of the day, such as Cecil Beaton and Lady Diana Cooper, Christopher Gibbs and members of the 'Chelsea Set'; artists David Hockney and Patrick Procktor, ballet star Wayne Sleep, the Beatles and the Rolling Stones, Brigitte Bardot, Marianne Faithfull, Liza Minnelli, Jeanne Moreau, Britt Ekland and marvellous models: Patti Boyd, Kellie, Carina Fitzalan-Howard, Amanda Lear, Gala Mitchell, Kari-Ann Moller, Verushka, Bianca Jagger. Everyone wanted to be there, but Ossie, as ever breaking the rules, did not put the press in front-row seats and only invited those people he liked. Nor did he cultivate powerful players who would have preserved his legacy for later generations, most particularly museum curators and members of

the fashion industry. There are too few examples of his work in museum collections in comparison with that of his contemporaries, and this has meant that his contribution to fashion has been somewhat overlooked. His focus was on making wonderful clothes, not on trying to ensure the posterity he deserves as a designer.

'I am as famous as Egg Fo Yung,' he wrote in his diary after the 1974 show at the Royal Court Theatre. But the painful separation from Celia Birtwell, whose talent and unerring taste had been a constant in his life, press that suggested that he should move on from his well-tried formula in recession-struck Britain and a reckless use of drugs contributed to making his work practice increasingly erratic. The latter years of his life were spent in the hope of returning to the fashion scene, and periods of highs and lows, although all the while he was still producing the most beautiful couture dresses for his friends.

Ossie drawing, 1970.

'I'm a master-cutter. It's all in my brain and fingers and there's no-one in the world to touch me. I can do everything myself. I can make a pair of gloves on a clamp between my legs, the proper way, holding a needle in each hand. I can make a bra. I can make a pair of shoes,' he told *The Sunday Times Magazine's* Georgina Howell in 1987. In the 1980s, however, it was the labels of the millionaire designers Calvin Klein, Giorgio Armani and Gianni Versace with their brilliant branding and advertising campaigns that were aspired to and worn, not the beautiful but small-scale work of a technical genius.

In 1994 there was evidence of a 1970s influence in fashion; two years before, he had given tuition to his friend Bella Freud's pattern cutter. [2] Linda Watson wrote in the *Evening Standard* of the desirability of 'vintage' Ossie. Supermodels Naomi Campbell and Susie Bick wore his clothes, as did fashion editor Suzy Menkes, who cherished her collection: 'Of all

above
Liza Minnelli and Jeanne Moreau
at a Quorum show, 1971.
Liza Minnelli wore an Ossie
red dress and a black-and-white
chiffon blouse with a Celia print
in the film Cabaret *(1972).*

opposite
Drawing by Celia Birtwell,
c. 1970.

the clothes that have passed through my hands or been on my body, his have given me the most pleasure.' Five years after his death, in its September 2001 issue, American *Vogue* discussed the legacy of his work in a trend piece, 'Almost Famous'. 'Who would have predicted that the king of King's Road would still be influencing high fashion in the year 2001?' It cited Prada's black dress and a sienna print, Louis Vuitton's polka dots and Dries van Noten's high-waisted dress with floral print as examples. 'He had a special talent for spinning strips of chiffon into ephemeral, fluid robes of frills and pleats. This year both Chanel and Christian Dior captured the look – which is sexily sheer…"He was the master of the bias cut," says admiring designer Anna Sui. "No-one created cascades of ruffles like he did. He dressed the woman we all wanted to be: the rock star's girlfriend."'

This book is a tribute not only to Ossie Clark but also to Celia Birtwell, whose sensitive and beautiful prints made his work so extraordinary. An exhibition at the Victoria and Albert Museum has never been so well deserved.

Judith Watt
January 2003

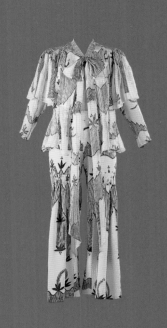

Manchester

'A very confident boy'

Ossie and friends, Manchester c. 1959.

Ossie Clark was born in Liverpool, on 9 June 1942, into a large, working-class family; his father, Samuel, had worked as the chief steward on a P&O liner. The youngest of six children, Ossie had been christened Raymond but was nicknamed after Oswaldtwistle, the Lancashire village to which the family was evacuated. After seven years they moved to the Cheshire town of Warrington, with its history of textile production, a magnificent Victorian municipal park and an art school. His mother, Anne, was an accomplished knitter who brought fabrics from Earlstown market. 'She was always artistic – at the age of eight she was knitting mufflers and jumpers, scarves and hats for the cannon-fodder that were being wiped out in Europe. She had a terrific colour sense and I'm sure I inherited a lot of my style from her,' he said. [3] She knitted jumpers for Ossie, which he loved and wore as an adult. At ten years old Ossie, too, was making clothes. He made

a bikini, and two years later, produced garments for his young niece and nephew.

This was all done in the privacy of home. At school, he failed his Eleven-plus exam and went to Beaumont Secondary School, where he excelled at mathematics, a talent that lay at the heart of his cutting skill. From there, he attended Beaumont Technical School, where he learnt building construction. 'We had teachers who taught us architecture. I actually learnt how to build walls using cement made with linseed oil instead of water so that it would never set. I learnt about geometry and I learnt how deep to make a foundation to build a wall so high.' [4]

At the same time that he was learning the difference between English and Flemish bond, his art teacher Roy Thomas was encouraging his latent drawing skills and inspiring in him a love of glamorous fashion. 'He was mad about fashion. He saw talent in me and he brought American *Vogue* and *Harper's Bazaar* and really

'**Sometimes a baby peers out of a pram with a face that implies that it has been here before and it knows the score. Ossie kept that face.**' Norman Bain

opposite
Ossie screaming, c. 1960.

nurtured an interest. He told my mother, "You've got a very talented child, Mrs Clark; he should go to art school."' [5] Thomas arranged for Ossie to attend classes at Warrington Art School every Saturday morning. He then got a place at the Regional College of Art in Manchester in 1958. He was taken on the strength of his talent alone – he had no portfolio but just a few drawings of ballet dancers and fashions inspired by Diana Vreeland at *Harper's Bazaar* and its rival, American *Vogue*. After a probationary term, he was accepted formally. His mother gave up smoking and took a job as a home help to finance her son. 'I was given the princely sum – it sounds unbelievable – of £6 8s.6d a term for a grant and a travel permit to go from Warrington to Manchester.' [6]

Two teachers, Miss Rider and Miss Tyrer, provided the vital encouragement and teaching he needed to develop his amateur skills and natural gifts. 'After a year really trying everything – hopeless at pottery, couldn't paint, had no

colour sense – I learnt how to thread a needle and sew and stayed until nine o'clock twice a week with a sweet tailor [Louis Huet], who came along after his business finished. And I remember crying after I made my first pair of trousers because when I put them on they went like a spiral around my legs. He showed me how you close the outside seam and you turn over, then you balance and mark.' [7] Ossie was learning the technical skills that became the foundation of his work.

A trip to London in 1959 to see Marlene Dietrich at the Queen's Theatre in Shaftesbury Avenue compounded his fascination with the glamour of the inter-war years that was evident in his later work. 'The curtain opened and she was standing in this wonderful dress that was completely see-through…she had this entire body made that fitted underneath it so that she appeared nude but in fact, her breasts were put in ice, her own hair was plaited away, the wig

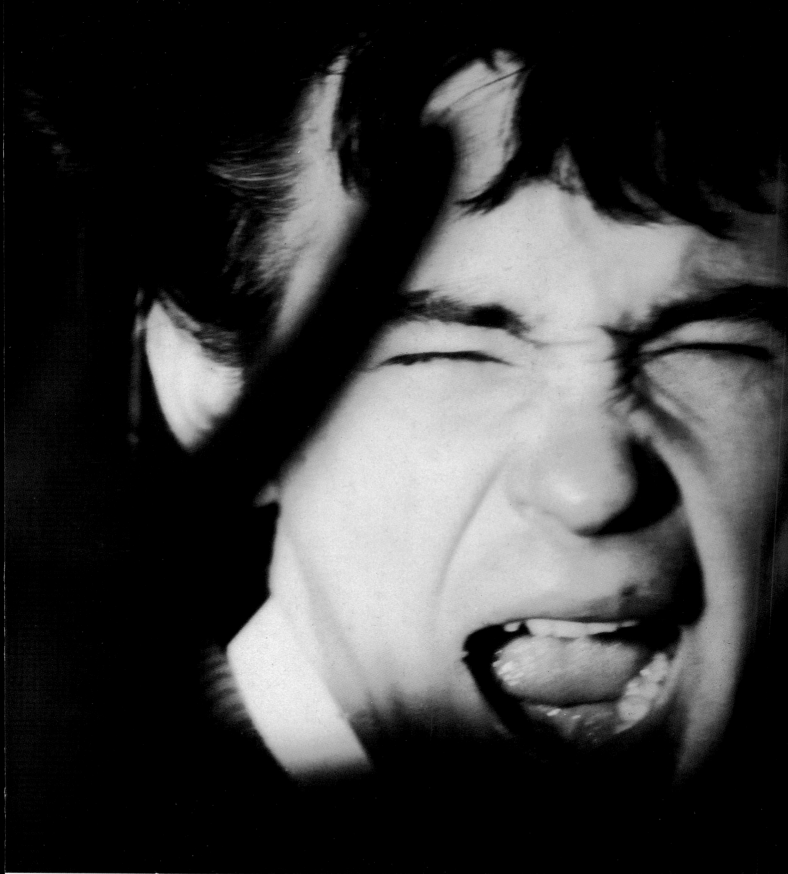

was perfect, she wore this fur coat with a three-metre train, and she sang "Look me over closely" and absolutely everybody did. She was truly incredible.' [8]

Like Dietrich, Diana Vreeland was of the older generation but also important to his notion of chic: 'Of all the stylish women I've met (and I've met quite a few), I would say she was the top dog. And she was in her 70s when I met her. She just was absolutely amazing. Full of youthful ideas and *joie de vivre* and nothing was too much trouble. Every morning she must have spent two hours on her appearance. *Maquillage*, hair – her hair was glossed black like a pair of guardsman's boots and her face was rouged.' [9]

Manchester, Salford and Bradford were all great northern towns whose wealth was based on wool and cotton; they provided an urban backdrop of 'little mean streets and back alleys', as Celia Birtwell described her college town of Salford, where L.S. Lowry would occasionally pop his head round the door of her studio. [10] It was this environment, however, that fostered the exotic talents of a group who would be seminal to the London art and fashion scene: Ossie with his penchant for Diana Vreeland; his fellow student, textile designer and artist Mo McDermott; and Celia, their friend, who was studying textile design at Salford College. Into this milieu came the young artist David Hockney, from Bradford but then completing his fine-art course at the Royal College of Art. 'We met at Manchester College of Art in 1961,' he says. 'A friend of mine who had been at Bradford was teaching at Manchester and I went to visit him and met Ossie. He was a very campy boy – I was rather attracted to his confident manner.' Pictures show Ossie as an impish, charismatic figure, dancing with girls he dressed in Quant-influenced pinafore dresses with short hems. His hairstyle had developed from a Lonnie Donegan quiff into a long cut, made widely fashionable of late by the Beatles.

Dress historian Valerie Mendes remembers seeing him at a party at the college: 'He was so beautiful, a little miracle in something pink.'

Ossie had met Celia in Manchester in 1960, through Mo McDermott. Celia remembers: 'Mo said, "There is this really mad boy" that I should meet. He had on a Beatle waistcoat cut in a vee, a Beatle shirt with the rounded collar and winklepicker shoes.' Born in Bury, Celia was brought up in Salford. 'I did have a very harmonious background; there was never very much money, but there was an educated father and a very practical mother, both Socialists, and their relationship was very strong,' she says. 'Father was an estimating engineer, but he should have been in a library – the house was full of books and flowers. He loved French Impressionist paintings so there were always nice things to look at. I was the eldest of three arty daughters. When it came to my life, I wanted to have something I hadn't experienced before. He was horrified when he found me listening to Elvis Presley on Radio Luxembourg!' Ossie first met Celia's parents in Salford on the night of the first screening of *Coronation Street*. Mrs Birtwell had trained as a seamstress, and helped Ossie make clothes. 'He liked my mother very much because she was extremely patient (unlike myself); she'd show him how to sew a collar or put a seam in,' Celia recalls. 'She had hours and hours of patience. She used to say to me, "He's really special." Or, "It's a work of art, Celia."'

His work at Manchester revealed a true talent for drawing and an ability to translate ideas into three-dimensional form. It was technical training rather than design and it equipped him with the skills of a master-cutter, as he later described himself. Although it has been said that he didn't 'discover' fashion history until he visited the Victoria and Albert Museum, two studies challenge this idea. One is a pair of costume studies in Indian ink of two

opposite

At a party at the Manchester Regional College of Art; Ossie's friend, the artist Mo McDermott is on the far left. 'In 1961 girls at art school were wearing the mini-skirt and had an extraordinary look that was five years ahead of its time.' This is one of his designs.

Reversible lounging
Culottes in pink
wrap printed and
deep purple/blue
taffetta. Embroidered
in the side pleats
of the purple side.
The culottes are
created into an undarted
hip band.

women from about 1468, probably copied from a manuscript illustration of the period that featured in a costume history book. The two full skirts, laced bodice and full sleeves are faithfully reproduced. This page shows his illustration for two trouser suits, with two full-bottomed trousers, which he described as 'bell-bottomed hipster trousers' and which were inspired by the shapes of the gowns in the manuscript. Although he was experimenting with ideas ahead of their time, his awareness of fabric and how it worked on the body was already evident. Jenny Dearden, who became a lifelong friend, and was later to work at Quorum, met Ossie when she was 14 and he 'adopted' her and made her clothes. One of his first commissions was to make the wedding dress for Jenny's sister: 'It was in very thick organza, very straight, with a narrow bodice and peplum. We went to the Woollands 21 shop and I bought a Foale and Tuffin keyhole dress

ROYAL COLLEGE OF ART   PHOTO

Submission of testimonies of study by applicants for admission to the Royal College of Art

Applicant's School of Art REGIONAL COLLEGE OF ART

Name of Applicant RAYMOND CLARK MANCHESTER

School of College to which admission is desired

THE FASHION SCHOOL

Brief description of testimony of Study DESIGN FOR

LOUNGING CULOTTES

Number of this Testimony 16   *Total Number Submitted* 25

RCA LABEL 1

above
*The completed RCA
application form. Note his real
name, Raymond.*

opposite
*Ossie's trouser suit designs, part of
his application portfolio for the
Royal College of Art, 1962.
Pen and ink on paper.*

to wear as the bridesmaid. Ossie wore a little collarless blue suit for the wedding.'

In order to learn about the fashion world, he undertook work experience at Christian Dior in Paris in 1960. The experience was formative: he was working at the most important House in the world, just as Marc Bohan had replaced Yves Saint Laurent. Fashion was at its grandest and most glamorous. 'Just so exciting to be crammed at the back of this huge salon and these exquisite clothes paraded in front of these wealthy women. And the last-minute hiccup while Barbara Hutton arrived with two Pekinese and then sat on a Biedermeyer couch and stopped the show every now and then, saying: "Divine! I'll have it in both colour-ways!", regardless of the price.' [11] It was light-years away from Manchester Regional College, combining perfectionism and elegance in the art of haute couture, which he adored.

Local press singled out Ossie – then

formally called Raymond – for attention. His work was now showing the influence of Pierre Cardin, who had revolutionized menswear with his *style anglais* launched that year and featuring a natural silhouette and traditional fabrics. In 1961, his second year, the local *Evening Chronicle* printed a picture of 'Raymond', the only man among 30 students on the course, with a Mod hairstyle and winklepickers (bought by Mo from 'Stan the man' for £6; they were too big), wearing 'a revolutionary man's suit with a collarless jacket, without buttons, lined with wild silk.' [12] It was in navy worsted, worn with a fawn suede waistcoat, and he modelled it himself in the annual fashion show. He told the *Daily Telegraph*: 'I want to concentrate on haute couture in Paris.' [13] Ossie was cleverly commercial; the collarless jacket, with a round collared shirt, was made even more popular by the Beatles in 1963, when it was dubbed a 'Beatle suit.'

In 1962 the *Drapers' Record* reported on a

'In Ossie's drawings you see the clothes immediately. They are very fluid and very precise and the clothes are very much like that.' Brian Harris

visit to the local manufacturer J. and M. Bartle's factory by final-year Manchester students, good news as far as the paper was concerned. 'The work of students in textile and clothing design although attractive was usually commercially impracticable. But I am told that this is much less true today…For one student, Raymond Clark, it was an opportunity to see a raincoat of his own design in production.' [14]

That year, his tutors encouraged him to try for the Royal College of Art in London (for which there was a strict age limit of 22). Fellow applicant Stevie Buckley met Ossie at the entrance exam, which lasted a week. 'People had come from all over the country to apply. He was a very willowy, little fey figure and came up to me and showed me one of his drawings of a dress. "It's clever," he said ingenuously, "and it crosses over and ties at the back like a pinny." It was really a straightforward little dress, but I thought, "Yes, I like you." Both of us got in

and we became friends.' Ossie was awarded a scholarship of £330 a year.

Once in London, Ossie met Celia again, who had gone there for a summer holiday and had stayed, working at Hades Coffee Bar ('very arty', she says), and at the Royal Shakespeare Company making wigs, 'dressed like B.B.,' Ossie recalled, 'blue jeans and Victorian blouse, boots with a lavatory heel.' Hockney had just graduated from the Royal College of Art and was seen as one of the hot young talents in London. He was living above Hennekey's pub on the corner of Portobello Road and Westbourne Grove, a centre of the contemporary art scene, where artists Peter Blake and Joe Tilson would drink. With Celia in Addison Road, Ossie had a group of friends who were already part of the London art and fashion scene in the capital's new bohemian area, Notting Hill.

overblouse made
in suede with
loose hip tie

Royal College of Art
Let the magic begin

The Fashion Design School at the RCA had been opened in the late 1940s by former *Vogue* editor-in-chief Madge Garland. She was succeeded as the School's head by Professor Janey Ironside in the late 1950s, by which time the RCA course had become the most prestigious in the country. The entrance exam included making toiles, patterns, design and a general knowledge test calculated to assess the applicant's creativity and imagination ('What does the word "scarlet" mean to you?'). This was followed by a searching interview. 'Janey made the final choice,' said Ossie. 'She saw that each one had a talent. It could be drawing or making clothes or it could just be ideas, or that they were passionate about a period in time.' [15]

Having been singled out for praise by local and national press and, in his own words, now 'the bee's knees', Ossie apparently seemed rather over-confident at his interview with Janey Ironside and Bernard Nevill. 'I thought that he

was a difficult character in the interview,' Nevill remembers. 'In those days, students were "anti" everything and it was difficult to teach them, I can tell you. They didn't want to be taught about "old-fashioned" things.' Ossie's friend Stevie Buckley thinks differently, however: 'He wasn't difficult, he was sharp. It was his defence when he *wasn't* feeling confident.'

Despite being of the older generation, Janey Ironside was pivotal to the course and to the students' development as designers. Ossie remembers her as 'a truly startling woman in her appearance and her mysticism. She was like a magic person; in the whole of the first year, we only saw her twice.' He recalls: 'She came in usually at about 11.30, always black and white with a gash of scarlet. Pale face, dark glasses, dyed black hair, and now I know, fortified with gin to face the students.' [16]

In her autobiography *Janey*, she described Ossie as one of her particularly talented

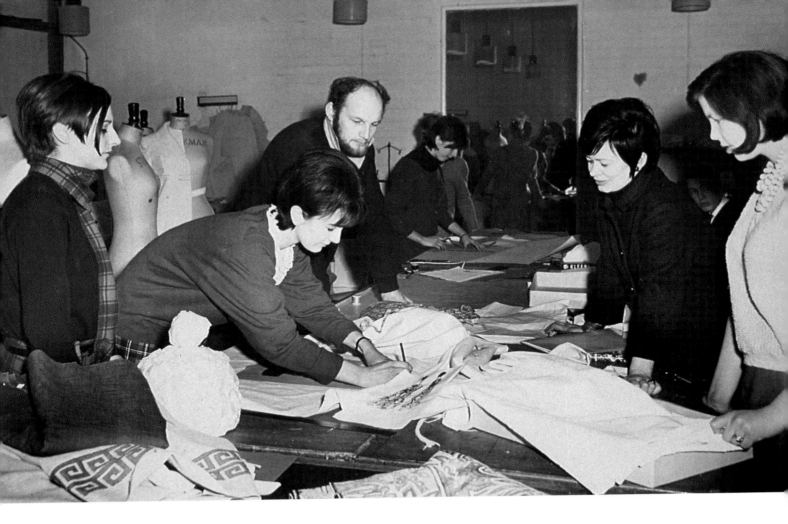

*Janey Ironside with
students, 1963.*
RCA Archive

students, interested in Pop ideas but who found inspiration in the past: 'Obviously very gifted from the beginning – his designs were already shadowing the 1930s and 1940s.'[17]

At the time, however, the trend was for clothes that were modern and looked to the present and future. 'If in the 1960s you were talking about 40 years previously, people would have gone to sleep,' says David Hockney. 'What was different, when people are doing a revival of the 1960s, was that the 1960s didn't do a revival of anything: that was the major difference. You felt a freshness that was exciting. You didn't let the commercial side interfere with things, in film, music, painting, fashion. It was an energy driven by the bohemian world.' All the fashion editors – Claire Rendlesham, Prudence Glynn, Meriel McCooey, Alison Adburgham and Suzy Menkes – looked to the RCA to spot the 'new Mary Quant' of British fashion.

Ossie described an incident that revealed the iconoclasm felt by his peer group when the couturier Hardy Amies, who also designed a very successful menswear line, came to give a talk. 'He brought with him some male models and his first collection of suits he'd designed for Hepworth's, the tailor. He said "You can criticize all you like, I don't mind." And so of course everybody laid into him and he didn't like it at all. And then he got rather insulting because at the time Marion Foale and Sally Tuffin had made a big success producing the kind of clothes that girls wanted to wear. They used Liberty's lawn, un-lined, which was shocking – that you could see through the body to the breast and the nipples. And they made trouser suits. Very marvellous, square-shouldered, wide-lapelled, narrow stove-pipe trouser suits that anybody who was anybody wore, and it was brilliant. For a woman to wear trousers then, apart from jeans and the sloppy-joe, which the

'Ossie had magic. His cutting was lovely and the femininity was brilliant; he understood women because he was very feminine himself.' Marion Foale

sculpture students would wear, was not on. Not on for another five or seven years.' [18]

The Fashion Design Course was taught by people in haute couture and mass market production, with lectures in history of art, philosophy and history of fashion. Roger Briné, who had a business in South Molton Street, taught tailoring and toiling on a stand, Mr Litman taught pattern cutting and Miss Elfer, dressmaking. Stevie Buckley remembers Mr Briné teaching them couture. 'He brought in a Balenciaga coat that we had to copy. Ossie came closest to it.' The fact that guest lecturers for complementary studies included Iris Murdoch, Marie Rambert and Buckminster Fuller bears testimony to the high standard of design education that made Britain the nursery for fledgling fashion designers. Students learnt millinery, shoe design, tailoring and belt-making, and they had life-drawing classes that improved their ability to create three-dimensional designs.

Marion Foale remembers returning to the RCA soon after launching her collection with Sally Tuffin. Ossie was on the childrenswear project that she was teaching there. 'He had a very engaging personality, rather beautiful, brown hair and bluey-grey eyes, slim with narrow shoulders. A look perfectly suited to the times.'

Vanessa Denza was the buyer for the Woollands 21 shop in Knightsbridge that had opened in 1961 and was then at the forefront of selling young British design. 'Everybody who was anybody was showcased there. Half of my involvement with that was that we found that we had no manufacturers who knew what we wanted,' she remembers. So she would buy directly from the designers, put the clothes on the rails and they would sell immediately. 'The turnover was phenomenal. We turned our stock every three weeks. We were in and out, in and out of new styles. We brought in new stuff all the time.' As such a vital figure, she was invited to lecture the fashion students. 'The first time I remember seeing him – how he had these glasses made I don't know but they were squared framed sunglasses – he was sitting in the back of the room,' she says. 'Remember that the number of MA students would never be more than about 15. So it was a very small group of people. If one student arrived who wasn't up to the standard we all wondered how that person had got through the net. There was no question of bums on seats as there is nowadays. You had to be bloody good to get in. Like racehorses, you know.'

In the late 1950s and early 1960s, when Hockney was still at the RCA, Londoners regarded themselves as the centre of new creativity; everything else was provincial. 'When I was at the RCA people would mock my accent. Ossie never had an accent, even when I first knew him. That was the beginning of the Beatles, so provincial England was in London. By then, it wasn't just seen as provincial, it was an energy. Ossie was from Manchester, I was from Bradford, Celia was from Salford.' The RCA was the place to be: Grace Coddington and Amanda Lear would model for the students, Ossie met the Rolling Stones' Charlie Watts in the bar. 'Every Friday there were dances at the bar full of non-RCA people, who wanted,' recalls Ossie's lifelong friend Norman Bain, who found himself dancing with Julie Christie one night, to be 'at the very centre of things.' Stevie Buckley explains: 'If [Ossie] was your friend, he was absolutely divine. We would go to the all-nighters at the RCA and dance to Georgie Fame. I remember going out with him once.

opposite
Fittings with Janey Ironside and Joanne Brogden, 1962.
RCA Archive

I was a bit plump and I'd made myself a black halter-neck dress in black linen. "You look just like Audrey Hepburn," he said. I was twice her size, but he was sweet to say it.'

Jenny Dearden, still living in Manchester, remembers that Ossie would send her presents, such as a pair of Pinet boots, which she wore with a red suede jacket that he had made for her. 'He loved the Royal. I think they recognized as soon as he got there that here was somebody special.' Ossie described the dress of those early years. 'What was extraordinary about the 1960s was that you have this androgynous thing, and the sexual freedom from the Pill and the fact that women could become the predator. There was one woman that we called the "Leopard Lady". There was a mound of hair and it was the same look. And she was always in a rush to get somewhere. With a yard of hair behind her. Long striding legs and lace stockings. She was truly incredible, a great inspiration. It was a wonderful time to be that age. I arrived in London at that time, and this whole sexual revolution went on. It didn't matter if you were a boy or a girl, you could be fancied by either sex. It was quite acceptable to accept an invitation to go out with Lionel Bart in his Rolls Royce, to go and have dinner with David Hockney or to go to Paris and see Madame Marthe and the transvestites, and to ask, "were they really men?"' [19]

Norman Bain, a year above Ossie, recalled him in his first year, making friends with people from each year, carrying his work with him from table to table as he chatted. 'He arrived from Manchester Art School with Jane Parker. Both were fluid and fluent in techniques.

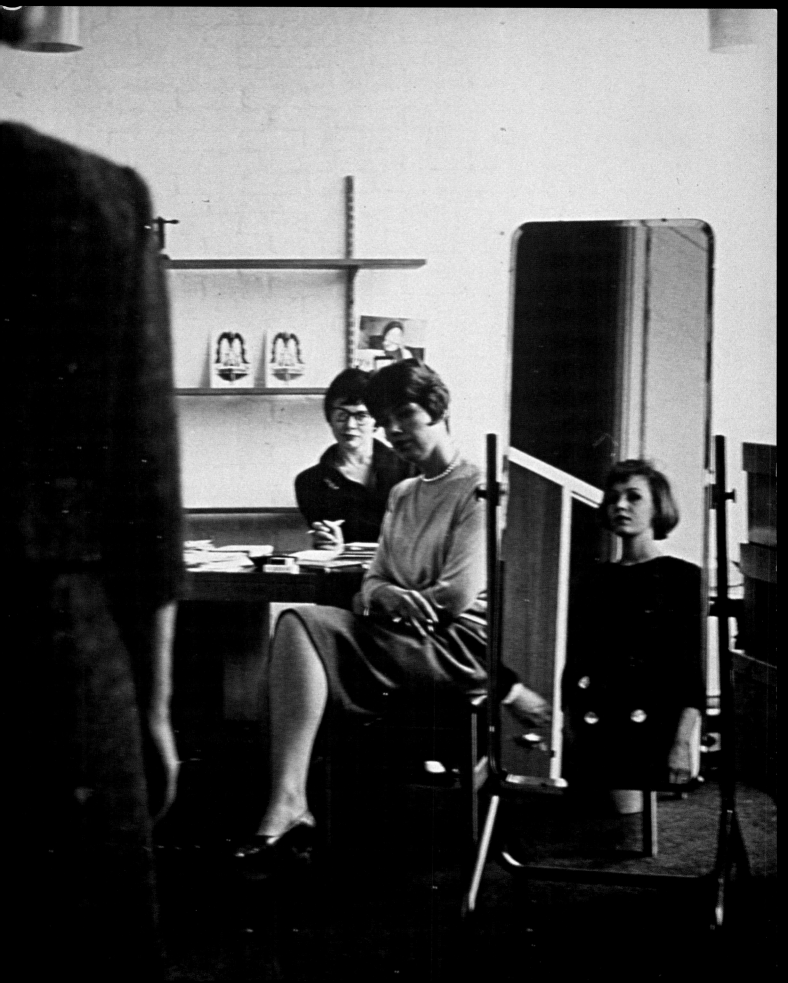

DINNER SUIT

above

above

Jacket and narrow trousers in cream silk. College project, 1964, and sold at Quorum in 1965–6. It is thought by those who were part of Ossie's world that this inspired Yves Saint Laurent to design his 'Le Smoking' suit of 1966.

opposite

Sample swatch of silk fabric for a jacket and trousers storyboard, 1964.

They could do anything. He would draw what he knew he could do and this had great scope, unlike most of us, who drew something and then discovered if it was or wasn't possible to realize. This kind of disappointment never happened to him. He was always serious and meticulous when designing and capable of great concentration and energy.' Nor was he afraid of the rules of cutting. He worked on new shapes that others did not have the imagination, or courage, to attempt. 'In his first year he completed his projects very quickly, then rushed off to explore London. He was always good fun, witty, but easily bored,' says Bain. Brian Godbold, another fellow student and friend, remembered that 'the thing about him then was that as students, we all used to work weeks on end, torturing some piece of fabric for a project. Ossie would put something together the night before and it would look untouched by human hands. He was a real natural.'[20] Ossie's older

sister Kay, a jazz singer, was already in London. The impression made by Dietrich, with her drop-dead costume, was not lost on him, and he made stage outfits for Kay that registered from a distance and made an impact on the audience, both important, as Bain points out, when putting on a fashion show. 'He always saw the woman and wanted her to look good.'

There are conflicting opinions, however, as to how technically competent Ossie was at the time. Concerned that he was lacking focus, Ironside had persuaded Gerald McCann, the commercial designer and couturier, to take him on. '"He's very rebellious and he reminds me of you," she said. This skinny little thing wearing a Greek sailorman's hat appeared at my studio in Lexington Street. I took him to lunch in Gerrard Street and he ate his way through half the menu. At the time I was very interested in Courrèges, and in 1962 had done a bra cut with a dress. I started talking about

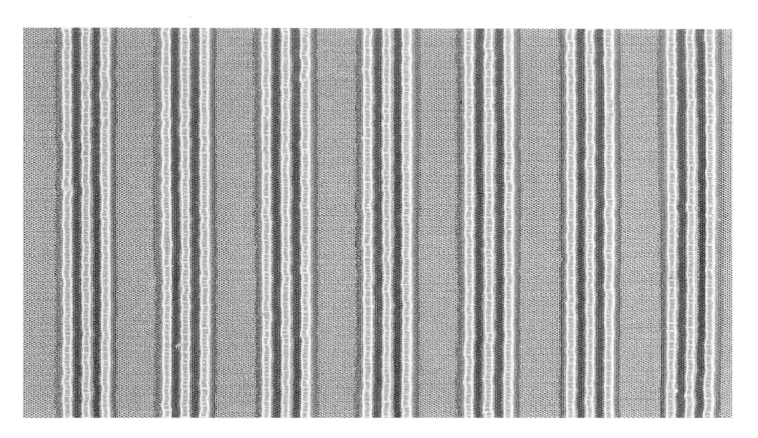

putting together lectures and he started taking notes. When he came to the studio, he couldn't cut a pattern.' Ossie left and didn't go back, although they were later friends. But couldn't cut a pattern? 'Oh, Ossie would wait and see how good someone else was before he would commit himself,' commented his seamstress, Kathleen Coleman. 'If he didn't want to do something, he just didn't do it.'

Perhaps it was the influence of Courrèges, an instrumental figure in launching unisex fashion, that did not appeal to Ossie. 'I like feminine clothes which make the girl more important than the dress,' he told a journalist in 1965. [21] He had already shown interest in the clothes and images of the past, and this came alive with the trips to the Victoria and Albert Museum. The writer James Laver, who had brought dress history into prominence, placing it in the context of art and social history, had been Keeper of the Department of Prints

and Drawings and Paintings there until 1959. The students were taken to the Museum to study by Bernard Nevill, who not only taught but was also a practising textile designer, historian and writer. He aimed to open the eyes of his students to the past and thereby demonstrate the huge possibilities of fashion design. 'I would take them to the V&A and ask Madeleine Ginsburg to get out all the old Schiaparelli toiles to examine the cut. They said they didn't want to look at "old-fashioned things."' He pointed out to them that what was so important about these 'old-fashioned things' was that Vionnet, Poiret, Chanel and Schiaparelli were all creating something new at the time, such as Vionnet's bias cut, which so informed Ossie's genre. This idea of the new spirit in dress made a connection with the students, themselves part of a moment when the contemporary – and the future – was exciting. For Ossie, however, this revelation of the past

Madeleine Vionnet backless dress,
American Vogue, *1937.*
Horst © Vogue/
The Condé Nast Publications Inc.

was completely inspiring. 'The year we spent with Bernard Nevill really opened all the students' eyes to the fact that fashion wasn't just rejecting everything your parents stood for, blackening your eyes and back-combing your hair and wearing white lipstick and high-heeled, pointed shoes and flared trousers, which all the students did. The mini-skirt which Mary Quant claimed to have invented – what about Egypt? What about the 1920s showgirl dancers?' [22]

'He was the most wonderful teacher,' Ossie said simply. Nevill set them a project to study one of the great couturiers: Lelong, Dior, Schiaparelli or Chanel. 'We went one afternoon a week to the Museum, and made careful copies of fashion illustrations from contemporary magazines and photographs. Then he showed us what inspired them, so we looked at Chinese pottery and Japanese wrapping-paper.' Norman Bain, who went through the same process, believes that those sessions, meticulously copying the fashion illustrations in the *Gazette du Bon Ton* by George Barbier, Georges Lepape or Charles Martin, and then having to illustrate in that style, were even more of an influence on Ossie than looking at clothes of the period. Ossie's favourite reading were the bound issues of *Vogue* kept in the studio, particularly those of the 1920s and 1930s, full of Madeleine Vionnet. 'The whole glamour thing of the 1930s, I think, was what influenced us,' thought Ossie. 'Whereas in the 1930s and 1940s satin bias, feather boas and lace were worn by goddesses of the screen, we thought: why can't people on the street wear them? So Bernard Nevill is directly responsible for that.' [23]

Norman Bain remembers the impact of certain films on Ossie's work. He particularly enjoyed these classes, and one of the biggest influences on his designing was a showing of the 1939 film, *The Women.* 'The first thing Nevill did was to arrange a showing. The story goes that it was made for all the actresses who didn't get the part of Scarlett O'Hara. The clothes were designed by Adrian and there's not a man in it. The clothes are exquisite. He showed us that Paris wasn't the be-all-and-end-all of clothing.' [24] This tension that he felt about Paris fashion was to be a theme that followed him through his life as a designer. Bain remembers him as a regular attendee of screenings at the Film Society, which showed classics such as *The Battleship Potemkin* (1925), 'interspersed with experimental works in which, for example, jewelled rosaries were filmed swinging in slow motion. Then the film was shown upside-down so they looked like glittering metronome-like trees swaying in the breeze. This film lasted for an eternity.' Another notable influence was *The Fugitive Kind* (1960), in which Marlon Brando and co-star Anna Magnani both wore snakeskin jackets; tailored snakeskin was to become one of the Ossie Clark hallmarks. In order to research the golden years of Hollywood, he bought Mae West's newly published diaries, and started writing one himself, a habit that he kept for the rest of his life. 'We loved Mae West,' says Norman Bain. 'Ossie, Celia and I would talk to each other in a Mae West voice for ages.' West was one of Ossie's all-time favourite women and her 'chutzpah' and curvaceous femininity were reflected by many of the women who wore and modelled his work. 'Fashion is now displayed on girls who haven't reached womanhood…you might as well put them on models made of wood…When the girl's got no breasts, no shoulder blades, no behind…I think for a garment to be successful it's got to flatter and it's got to be comfortable.' [25]

Fellow student Hylan Booker described those days to Henrietta Rous, who edited the Diaries. 'As a student he was always so good and pulled one's own standards up, even if his

attitude did not always conform. Janey Ironside
had a special relationship with her students –
it was very personal, very warm, very open.
We blossomed because we were encouraged.
She was quiet and authoritative. It was
extremely stimulating because we had such
talented students – Janice Wainwright, Zandra
Rhodes, Sally Tuffin and Marion Foale; John
Bates the milliner and James Wedge came in as
instructors…Ossie was a rebel and pooh-poohed
conventions. Within our year he was the most
excellent pattern-cutter. He was brave, fabulous,
debonair and witty; he was always able to say
something sardonic but he was bursting with
talent. He was also incredibly competitive
– he was a true designer and had great
confidence.' [26]

There was another very important
influence: Celia Birtwell. From being friends,
they became lovers, living together in
Westbourne Grove, Notting Hill, all the time
she was working on her textile designs. The
possibilities open to them as a team must have
become apparent at this time. 'He was highly
talented and creative,' she says. 'He could have
been an architect. He would find lovely things,
he loved buying glass vases, had a very good
eye. This talent then started and we could work
together, he on shapes, me on colour.' Dressing
like Brigitte Bardot, with cat-like eyes, blonde
hair, small and slim, a tiny waist and round
bosom, she was devastatingly pretty. Her shape
was distinctly female at a time when fashion
models were becoming increasingly boyish, and
she was to be his muse. They travelled to Paris
together, and went to Chanel, where they were
invited by the *vendeuse* to take a seat and watch
a client at a final fitting. 'They were much more
concerned about the sleeve and she was not at
all bothered about the sleeve, as far as she was
concerned the sleeve was perfect. Then we saw,
in the mirrors of the spiral staircase, Madame

opposite
*Celia and Ossie at his
flat in East Putney, 1967.*
© **Norman Bain**, 1967

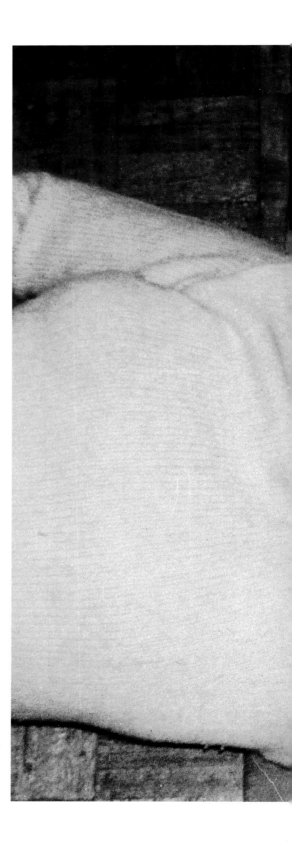

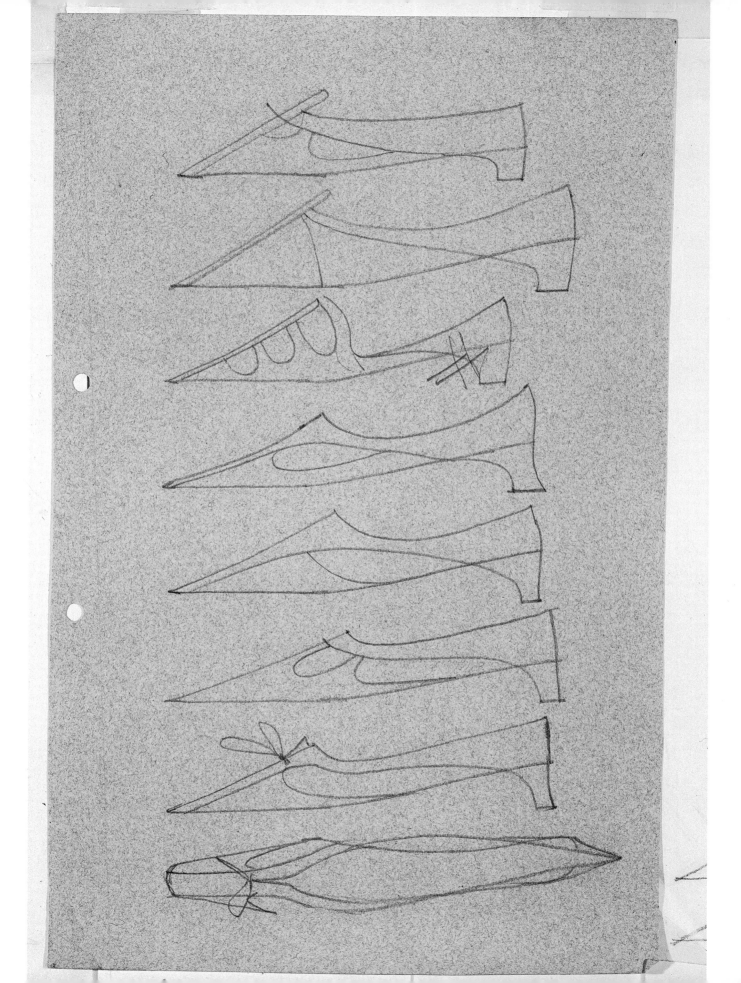

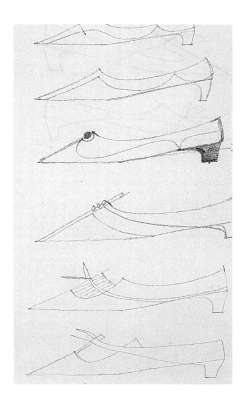
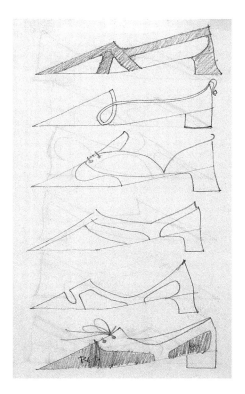
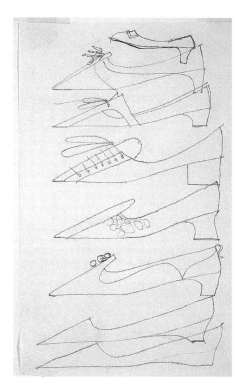

A small selection of Ossie's winning shoe designs for the Down Shoes factory competition, 1964.

Chanel herself sat looking. Taking it all in and watching. It was a great honour to see her.' Ossie was also influenced by Pierre Cardin 'who made this collection of clothes which was mad but wonderful. Chiffon dresses which were short at the front and long at the back. The models sort of ran on and the hats were like sou'westers made of chiffon and there was this spiral line which, again, influenced me later on.' [27]

Norman Bain knew them both, and took some of the earliest photographs of them together. He recalls that, having enjoyed himself in the first year, Ossie began to blossom in his second year (1963–4). 'It was in his second year that his talent became noticeable and he spent longer on his work. He entered *The Sunday Times* annual fashion competition with drawings for womenswear, and at the last minute, dropped in a few menswear designs. It was the menswear designs that won him a prize. Ernestine Carter, the paper's fashion editor, thought my entry

was the first garment based on Pop Art. Whether or not it was, it had a hat that I was dreading to make. Ossie looked at the sketch, a huge blue tweed floppy affair with long trailing nun's veiling bands with large numbers tumbling over it, and offered to make it for me. He followed my sketch to the letter. No designer tantrums. It looked wonderful and it was a very kind gesture that I never forgot.' Ossie's versatility was further demonstrated when he won a competition for shoe design in 1964. The bursary was £150 and he worked at the Down Shoes factory in Banbury, Northern Ireland.

As well as David Hockney (with whom he had a brief affair), his friends included young artists Patrick Procktor and Howard Hodgkin, art student Derek Jarman, dancer Wayne Sleep, and fellow fashion student Bill Gibb and his boyfriend Kaffe Fassett. 'In those days,' says Hockney, 'he would overlap with the art world, the characters were similar.

'He had an attitude
to form, which
is instinctive to
artists.' David Hockney

David Hockney,
c. 1969.

It certainly seemed to be more bohemian
[than now], and most people liked that.'

In 1964, Hockney taught a summer term at
Iowa, and Ossie, with his £150 prize, went to
America with him, flying to Chicago and
driving to Los Angeles. 'Route 66 – driving
along it, listening to England's latest hit makers,
the Rolling Stones,' Ossie later wrote. [28]
He met Bette Davis and Dennis Hopper in Los
Angeles; Brian Epstein gave him tickets for the
Beatles' Hollywood concert, where he was
mistaken for George Harrison. In New York
he met *Vogue*'s editor-in-chief Diana Vreeland,
Andy Warhol and the Velvet Underground,
and the artist Robert Indiana gave him a bolt of
Op Art material printed with his design, which
Ossie was to use in his degree collection. On his
return, he moved in with Celia at her flat in St
Quintin's Gardens, North Kensington, with the
white cat Blanche, named by Norman Bain after
Blanche Dubois, and Beulah, the little black

poodle, her name inspired by Mae West's line,
'Beulah, peel me a grape.' 'I would spend
Saturday evenings with them before they all
went to a party. Celia would cook some supper,
then we'd sit down to eat and they'd both start
drawing together in their books. Ossie might
spend a couple of minutes completing a really
difficult Chinese puzzle, play music, but
basically, they would sit and draw.'

His MA collection was Op Art and Bridget
Riley influenced, using the black-and-white
fabric Robert Indiana had given him, PVC
and suede. Even at that stage, he said that he
found the cloth was the springboard for a
design. Students were officially allowed to
present six garments for their degree collection,
which had to be within a fixed amount; the
rules were sometimes flexible, however, and
the Robert Indiana fabric, certainly way over
budget, was allowed. One of the pieces was an
evening dress, bias cut, with thin straps,

showing the direction in which he was to go – turning eveningwear into daywear. Bain remembers the process of that hard year well. 'For the final fittings, students queued up nervously, outside Professor Ironside's office. Once inside, you sat with three other students on a sofa at one end, each clutching a garment and its sketch. In the middle of the room stood the fitter/technician, Mr Polaris, and at the far end behind her desk sat Janey Ironside. She managed to balance authority with sympathy and very sure judgement. Her aim was to help you to do the very best you could in your own style. When she said "I don't think this is working, do you?", you knew it was not a question.'

The textile designer Natalie Gibson was present at the degree show in June 1965, held at the Gulbenkian Hall. 'It was the days when you would have a wedding dress at the end of the collection: Ossie made a huge white dress with fairy lights, very magical.' He claimed to have been influenced by Léon Bakst, who had designed a costume for Diaghilev's Ballets Russes that lit up with lightbulbs. In the collection was a pink suede jacket with trousers, and the Op Art dress with its plunging neckline featured a scarf at Janey Ironside's insistence, to make it 'decent'.

He graduated with a first-class degree, the only one of his year, and was selected by *Vogue* to appear in an article on young designers in the August issue. 'I want to dress frilly people…in colours that confuse the eye,' he told the readers. [29] Norman Bain was at hand to help. 'After Ossie's tour-de-force collection, he was summoned to *Vogue* to be photographed by David Bailey. He was instructed to wear a black polo-neck sweater. He didn't have one and couldn't afford to buy one. He remembered that I used to wear one in what I fondly thought of as my French existentialist phase and I lent it to him although I was twice his size.

above
Design for a suit.

right
*Two figures wear trousers
and tunic tops.*

opposite above
*Black-and-white dress, bias cut,
fabric by Robert Indiana.*

opposite below
*Pink dress with large white
spots and a cotton swatch.*

**Ossie's designs for his degree
collection, 1965.**

Ossie with Chrissie Shrimpton,
who wears his quilted coat in
Robert Indiana Op-Art fabric.
Vogue, *August 1965.*
David Bailey © Vogue/
The Condé Nast Publications Ltd

Ossie's fashion drawing for
the same coat, a gift
for Norman Bain, 1965.
Pen on paper.

'What Ossie and Alice summed up articulated the freedom of what was going on and they did this through clothes.' Fiona Ronaldson

opposite
*Alice Pollock photographed for
'My Day by Alice Pollock'.
'Spent the first hour talking to
Celia Birtwell. We had many
things to discuss. The new
Hampstead shop, colours
and fabric for next season,
plus domestic things such
as children, holidays and the
problems of house-hunting.'
Vogue, September 1972.*
**Vogue/The Condé Nast
Publications Ltd**

When he returned it there were marks where it had been clipped to make it fit. It was an excellent photograph, with Ossie standing beside a model [Chrissie Shrimpton, then Mick Jagger's girlfriend] wearing his quilted Op-Art coat. He gave me the original drawing of the coat as a slightly guilty "thank-you" present.'

'He made his mark at the Royal College with his electric-lightbulb coat. People started talking about that. That was what really put him in the picture,' says Vanessa Denza, who bought his first collection for Woollands 21. An article in the *Sunday Mirror* by Shirley Lowe, '2 Names Make a Gold Label Breakthrough', featured Hylan Booker and Ossie as 'dress designers' with a 'Label'.[30] Ossie was pictured standing next to a model wearing a crêpe shift dress, its subtly flared hemline just above the knee, at 11 guineas for Woollands 21. 'I want to aim for the one per cent of the public who are on the same wave-length as me. These days you

can go to a party, look around, and because the clothes are so individual you can see designers instead of girls,' he told *Mirror* readers.

Terrified of launching on his own, because, unlike Booker, he hadn't got the 'chat', Ossie was reported as having just signed a contract with a manufacturer to design a spring collection under his name, and that he was working with a 'small Kensington boutique.' He had met another young designer, Alice Pollock, the previous year, at the opening of Quorum furnishings and fashion – a 'small Kensington boutique' in Ansdell Street, and she invited him to design for her.

'The Wizard of Ossie'

Portrait of Ossie Clark, one of a triptych.

Alice Pollock opened Quorum in 1964 with two friends and one hundred pounds. With Foale and Tuffin, Mary Quant and Barbara Hulanicki, who had just opened Biba in nearby Abingdon Road, Kensington, all catering for the needs of the new generation of women, it was open season for youth fashion. Born on 9 June 1942 in Southern Rhodesia, the daughter of a mining engineer, Alice had been brought up from the age of nine by her grandmother, in the Shropshire county town of Shrewsbury. She was untrained as a designer – she had just finished working as PA to Tony Richardson on the film *Tom Jones* – but she could make clothes. 'I had to do something to pay the rent…I didn't think: "I'm going to be a dress designer and become rich and famous." I just wanted something to do,' she later told a journalist. 'We made a range and called up the magazines. The first one to give us a break was *Queen*. Then we took over the shop beneath us. But it was still very

homey. It didn't become professional till Ossie joined us.'[31] Alice's first backer had been the theatre producer Michael White; his wife was one of their designers until she became pregnant and left. It was through Alice's second backer, Michael Armitage, that she had met Ossie: 'So young, so small, so shy, and so we began our curious relationship.'[32]

For Ossie, the meeting with Alice was momentous. He told Celia that he had met an 'incredible girl,' another Gemini (like many in the 1960s, he was a firm believer in astrology). 'I think that she's an amazing person and she wants me to design for her.' In 1965, he joined Quorum, first as designer, then partner. While she kept on another designer, Charlotte Flood, she asked Ossie, then living with Celia in St Quintin's Gardens, to design one print; Celia went ahead and did a fabric collection, and from there, the collaboration between Celia and Ossie formally began, with the prints acting as

above

Ossie and Suki Poitier,
who is wearing a Celia-print
'floating daisy' dress in
moss crêpe at Quorum,
Radnor Walk, c. 1967–8.
Carinthia West and Kathleen
Coleman are behind them.

motivation for many of his designs. 'He'd say, "Do whatever you like and I'll work with them,"' she remembers. Then he would show her his drawings and discuss the feasibility of combining the two. Stevie Buckley remembers: 'Celia didn't draw fabric designs flat because they were on little figures. So it was a combination of both of their talents; not only was he inspired by her work, but also by the way in which she put it on a body.'

Celia had been filling her sketchbooks with what she calls her 'fantasy girl' since she was a child. This ideal girl, who looked remarkably like her, with soft curling hair and Cupid's-bow lips, sloping shoulders and a noticeable bosom, became a reality between them. 'It was unique, because one always has an ideal in mind and it was my idea of what was pretty,' she says in retrospect. Alice also asked Celia to create two designs for her. Both were border prints, one a Cubist-inspired design, the other of tulips

climbing up the dress from the hem. 'My father always loved gardens and flowers. "There is so much in Nature," he would say. "Why look at anything else?"' These floral designs were very much part of the English tradition of embroidery and prints, which she would see at the National Art Library at the Victoria and Albert Museum. Like Ossie, Alice would give her a free rein. 'Not many people say that to you in life.'

Soon moving to Blenheim Crescent, W11, close to Portobello Road, Ossie and Celia would trawl the market, buying flowers, LPs, china and clothes from the 1920s, 1930s and 1940s. It was on one of these trips that Ossie bought a 1930s dress and began experimenting with the bias cut. He developed his style at Quorum, working with and supported by Celia and Alice. Leslie Poole, a cutter and friend since their RCA days, defines the importance of this new phase. 'I always felt at the RCA that he expressed the

above left
*Drawing in a sketchbook,
c. 1969. Ossie's tightly fitting
culottes and Rocker jacket were
typical Chelsea Girl wear.*

above right
*Ossie 'Hoopla' dress for Quorum,
influenced by American designer
John Kloss, 1966.*
Collection of Celia Birtwell

young talent of the period. But when he went to Quorum he changed the form of cutting which, in the post-war period, had been very influenced by Dior.'

In 1965 and 1966, his work chimed naturally with the look of the moment – such as his 'Hoopla' dresses – short sleeveless mini-dresses in blue wool with geometric inserts in orange and white at the bust, launched in 1966. Like Janice Wainright, whom he admired (and for whom Celia produced Op-Art designs), and Foale and Tuffin, he was influenced by the American designer John Kloss, whose cutting was based on geometrical shapes without darts. The 'Hoopla' dress was modelled by Patti Boyd, and *Vogue* featured this and a sleeved mini-dress, modelled by Twiggy in its 'Young Ideas' section (November 1966). 'Three-colour knits with geometric dimensions, rip-rap stripes of pink and purple, Ossie Clark for Quorum…9gns each,' wrote the section's editor, Marit Allen. [33]

In the spring that year Ossie had his first fashion show, held on a barge in Little Venice. This first collection was a moderate success with buyers, selling to Henry Bendel in New York and attracting important press; Prudence Glynn of *The Times* and Molly Parkin, fashion editor of *Nova*, the new (and cleverest) women's magazine, were impressed. Parkin saw the second Quorum show and in 1967 asked him to design a paper dress. It was short and simple, but Celia's print of orange and green flowers is reminiscent of designs produced by Poiret's Martine workshops and was very new for the time, an exciting indication of the Art Deco influence that was to be the feature of some of her most successful patterns. It was their love of the earlier 20th-century Orientalism and the inspiration they took from it that was to set their work apart from their peers.

Candida Lycett Green, daughter of Poet Laureate Sir John Betjeman and his marvellous

*Ossie and Celia stand in front of
the paper dress design commissioned
by* Nova *magazine in 1967.*
© **Norman Bain**

Celia's design for the paper dress commissioned by Nova.

wife Penelope Chetwode, remembers going to Ansdell Street for the first time. 'I first saw Ossie's clothes when I went shopping for my trousseau for my honeymoon; my parents had given me the money to shop around. It had been decided that a couturier should do my wedding dress (in which I think I looked awful) but I went into Quorum. It was down a cobbled alley. I walked in and saw the most magical frock I'd ever seen. It made me look very slim and I bought two, I think they were £18 each,

above

*Ossie's fashion drawing
for a beach top and trousers,
and for a full-length sleeveless
tweed cardigan, c. 1966.*

which was an incredible amount – I was used to paying about £8.' She married Rupert Lycett Green, owner of the tailor's Blades, in Savile Row, the first person to bring fashion to that august arena. She soon met Ossie at one of their supper parties at their house in Chepstow Villas, at the smart end of Westbourne Grove, when he accompanied David Hockney to one of their eclectic evenings. 'At that stage there was so much artistic talent buzzing around in that area,' she remembers. 'I just loved him – we had an instant rapport. He had a slim-hipped sexiness like Mick Jagger, the same sinuous fluidity. He was flirtatious; you definitely had the feeling of bisexuality, and that was an attractive quality. He didn't appeal to debs – their mothers wouldn't have approved of Ossie's look. He was very witty and you felt proud that he liked you, because he could be quite vituperative in a funny way. I was attracted by his talent.'

Frances Ronaldson, who designed textiles for Alice in the early 1970s (and married her ex-husband, Nick Pollock), is emphatic about the importance of Quorum, and the role of Alice in particular. 'It was the beginning. British fashion was on a roll, being promoted in *Vogue*. We were all in there, it was magic, the energy that it created was fantastic, no-one had ever done it before. It set the precedent for London being the centre for ideas. The King's Road was like a *passaggiata*.' In the autumn of 1966, Quorum moved to 52 Radnor Walk, off the King's Road, the centre of London's high fashion and home of the 'Chelsea Set': aristocratic bohemian style-makers such as Christopher Gibbs, David Milinaric, Mark Palmer, Julian Ormsby Gore and his sister Jane, married to Michael Rainey, owner of the men's fashion boutique, Hung on You, and Nigel Waymouth, owner of the super-trendy King's Road boutique, Granny Takes a Trip.

English Boy models in Chelsea,
one wearing Ossie Clark.
Owned by Sir Mark Palmer
and Alice Pollock, English Boy
was the most fashionable
of all the model agencies.
Both Marisa Berenson and
Peter Hinwood were on its books.

José Fonseca, who ran the model agency English Boy owned by Mark Palmer and Alice Pollock (and later opened the model agency Models One), remembers: 'I used to work as the hat-check girl at the Casserole restaurant on the King's Road; Ossie would come in and I met him there. There weren't many places to eat in the King's Road and it was very trendy. Nureyev and David Bailey used to eat there. Chelsea was like a village then, full of artists and cheapish accommodation, so it was a magnet for people.' Christopher Gibbs believes: 'There was an unfurling moment. When, as my friend Jane Rainey once said, "Do you remember when we used to walk down the King's Road and if anybody looked wonderful we knew them?" It coincided with the beginning of the Rolling Stones and the Beatles and the beginnings of LSD and all those hallucinogens. The famous breaking down of the barriers that was going on then.'

As part of that unfurling moment, Ossie became friends with Christopher Gibbs, then writing a column for the new 'Men in Vogue' section of *Vogue* and mythologized by Nik Cohn in his *Today There Are No Gentlemen* (1971). He was an aesthete and antiquarian, an important catalyst at that time, bringing together people disparate in age and background, such as Mick Jagger and Keith Richards with Cecil Beaton and Lady Diana Cooper. All were united in their desire to be part of the action and the energy of the mid-1960s, but in Ossie, Gibbs recognized something deeper and more serious. 'Ossie was such a different kettle of fish. He was an aesthetical creature who saw beauty in some unexpected places and people, and tried to harness the essence of what he saw. Other people were good hustlers, with a false kind of energy and charisma. Ossie was not a hustler. It wasn't his thing. He came up with some people who were very gifted as well, like Hockney and Patrick Procktor, but they were his friends.

For Ossie with love.

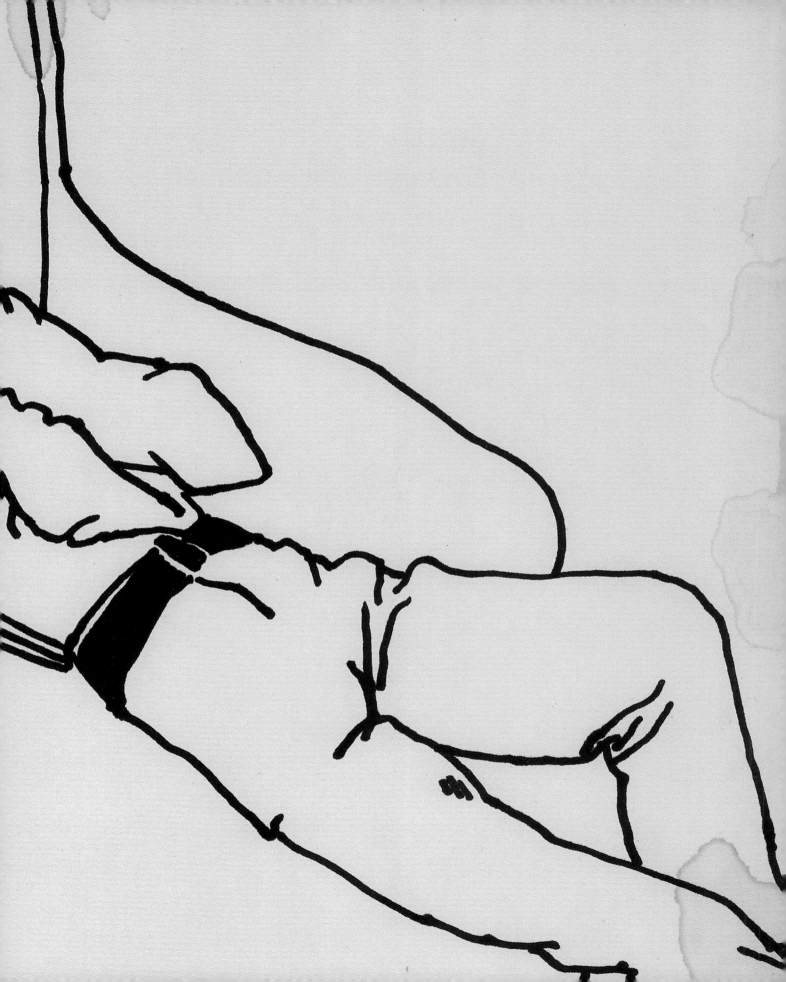

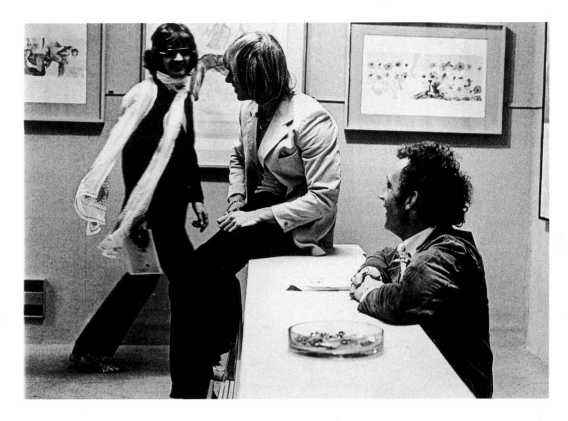

They weren't trying to learn from each other how to clamber up the ladder. It was another world.'

That same year, 1966, Gibbs, Ossie and friends went to Morocco to stay in his house in the mountains. Gibbs remembers the observational powers of his friend. 'He looked at everything always. And I remember him looking at the local people, who didn't have much at all, who made clothes out of a few bits and pieces. How they did it all with just a few knots. The colours were faded and subtle. He found that interesting.' This was the Orient in reality and was to influence his chiffon designs in their tying and the fabulous mix of colour and pattern created by Celia. Boutiques such as Michael Rainey's wonderful Hung on You, which had opened in 1965 in Cale Street, off the King's Road, would use Moroccan and Eastern fabrics for clothes and interiors; Ossie filtered this through his own design process and

created something new.

Later in 1966, as a reaction against the shape that concealed the waist, Ossie started working on a look that sculpted the body and made fitted black leather jackets, dubbed 'Rocker' for both sexes, and culottes for women which concealed the legs, so recently exposed by the mini-skirt. The black leather jackets, associated in the popular mind with Rockers and a gay aesthetic ('at the time, remember, homosexuality was illegal' points out Hockney), moved out of subculture and into fashion. He discovered in a warehouse, possibly owned by Alma Leather, rolls of untouched python and watersnake skins. Ossie, who had been horrified by the image of dead sheep being dragged by one leg in preparation for the annual feast of the sheep in Morocco, did not, like the majority of people at the time, have a horror of using leather, fur or skins. '"What's that?" I asked, touching the gentlest touch to the skin of a 26-inch python

when the train left the station

above

One of Ossie's holiday snaps of Yves Saint Laurent and friends in Marrakech, 1966.

opposite

Ossie's snakeskin Rocker jacket, c. 1966–7.
'The revolutionary thing was using python skin, no-one else had done that, and we used pearlized leather, too. They were made up by Mr Kent in Streatham, a leather-maker, who made a leather jacket for Peter Hinwood.'
Collection of Celia Birtwell

lain rolled for 20 years. "How much?" I asked, but matter-of-fact, hiding my enthusiasm. "Let's see, er, I can do that for 30 bob a foot" (glad to get shut). It was so wide I made it into a suit and Linda Keith [Jimi Hendrix's girlfriend] modelled it.'[34] Coats were made for Britt Ekland, Verushka and Twiggy, who wore her snakeskin coat trimmed with arctic fox on her New York tour in 1969.

The shiny watersnake jackets were constructed in diagonal strips of skin which fitted the body perfectly – and they were a first. Jenny Dearden comments on his constant quest for originality in relation to the influence of other designers on his work: 'I can't remember him referring to anybody. No. If he referred to anybody it would be to some one from the past, like Vionnet or Charles James. Certainly not to anybody current, any of his contemporaries. Quite the reverse. They would sneak into the shop or get somebody to go in and take stuff

away. Somebody from Saint Laurent definitely came. I worked in the shop then. In his next collection there was a little Rocker jacket that he'd done and also the smoking jackets that he started. He'd just look at the picture in the press and say nothing; of course he didn't like it.' Marit Allen at *Vogue*, who had met him that year when she featured the 'Hoopla' dress, agrees: 'In 1966–7, Ossie was creating new proportions, putting biker jackets with skating skirts at lengths no-one else was doing. After that, Yves Saint Laurent did biker jackets.' In 1966 she arranged for *Vogue* to feature a fashion editorial on Ossie, the first time *Vogue* had solely featured a young British designer. Shot by Norman Parkinson, Jean Shrimpton wears the Rocker jacket, priced at 15 guineas, and culottes, the 'uniform' of the Chelsea Girl.

Adie Hunter, who took over Quorum's PR from Chelita Secunda in 1970, describes the 'Chelsea look' of the early period: 'Hung on You

above left
Gala Mitchell wears a blue
and white silk chiffon dress with
a lily print. The photograph is
by Celia, taken at their home,
55 Linden Gardens.

above right
Celia's drawing of the famous
blue lily pattern, printed on silk
chiffon and cotton velvet.

was for the boys and Ossie for the girls.
We would have a black leather jacket and culottes,
chiffon skirt and something floaty at night…Shoes
by Chelsea Cobbler, patent leather shoes with
kitten heels, or black suede with ties up the legs
and light shoes for the chiffon dresses.' Jean
Shrimpton would visit him in Quorum. 'In the
1960s, we had a completely different attitude to
life from that of today; we were not a materialistic
generation. His clothes were very feminine and
comfortable, that bit different. I bought lovely
cardigans with puffed sleeves and ribbing at the
waist – they reminded me of the things I'd worn
in childhood and elicited a response. Both Celia
and he were so talented. The irony was that
I wasn't that interested in clothes even though
I was a model. Anyone who makes things that
make models look beautiful is sympathetic to
them and to women.'

Ossie developed new ready-to-wear designs
that were sold in the boutique throughout the

year; as with Quant and the other British
designers, the shop was the primary forum for
presenting new ideas. In 1968, Saint Laurent
opened his ready-to-wear Rive Gauche boutique
in London with Lady Rendlesham – influenced
by the British model that had made high fashion
accessible and an exciting shopping experience.
Unlike Saint Laurent, however, Ossie did not
have the power of a great fashion House behind
him, or the support of a Pierre Bergé, with the
formal structure of haute couture collections
twice a year. This was to become increasingly
problematic over the years, as his lifestyle
became more erratic with drug use. In Paris,
it was far more likely that he would have been
financially and emotionally supported as his
talent decreed. 'The thing about the Chelsea
Set,' says Norman Bain, 'is that they always had
a country house to go back to.' But Ossie had
fantastic back-up at Quorum, primarily from
Alice Pollock, who was prepared to nurture him

Pale Blue
suede
Different colours.
9

Ossie's drawing for a suede jacket, annotated with 'pale blue suede' in his writing. From his time at the RCA, he loved working with skins, whether leather, snake or furs, and suede featured in his womenswear, in conjunction with marocain and other fabrics.

at the expense of her own creative output.

'Alice was a major force, a major designer too,' says Frances Ronaldson. 'She had this business with this other girl and they were producing really well cut, nice dresses with Liberty prints and it was all starting up, and then Ossie came along and the other girl I think disappeared. Ossie taught Alice a lot about cutting and they worked together. Basically she protected him – sometimes he just couldn't be bothered with it. She had a good business mind. He owes much of his success to her. Alice negotiated with people and dealt with Ossie in her own way because she was similar to him. She was the go-between that enabled him to produce his work. And in those days it was always 'Ossie Clark and Alice Pollock', they were spoken of in one phrase.' Her sister Fiona Ronaldson describes the difference between wearing an Ossie and Alice dress. 'If you were feeling great and put on an Ossie Clark, you'd

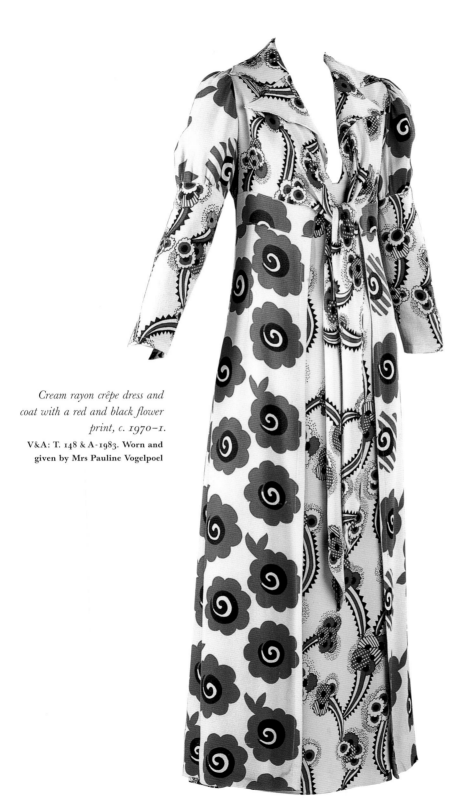

*Cream rayon crêpe dress and
coat with a red and black flower
print, c. 1970–1.*
**V&A: T. 148 & A-1983. Worn and
given by Mrs Pauline Vogelpoel**

feel a million dollars. If you felt awful and put
on an Alice Pollock you'd look fabulous. Ossie
made result-wear. He made women feel and
look sexy.'

In 1966, a young technician, Tony Costelloe,
who had been making accessories for Biba in
a building opposite the Radnor Walk shop, was
made redundant. Alice found him working on
a building site nearby and suggested that he
should join Quorum. 'She asked, "Have you
ever cut clothes?" She showed me a knife-cutter
and said "I'm sure you'll learn." She was a
fabulous catalyst for people,' he says,
affectionately. Then he was introduced to
Ossie. 'He was very laid back, with a lot of
common sense. When I told him that I wasn't
a trained cutter he just said, "Lay the pattern
on the fabric." I cut it and he saw that I could
do it. I picked up things as I went along.
Kathleen Coleman would help and the
machinists would cut things, too.'

Kathleen Coleman had been trained at
Harrods and at Marshall and Snelgrove, and
joined Quorum in Ansdell Street as a sample
machinist in 1965. 'I was 26 and only went
there to earn money for a holiday. My first
impression was that Ossie was very good, very
friendly. We cut and made all the dresses there,
taking only small orders and selling in the shop.
Then we moved to Radnor Walk.' She stayed,
working out the designs with Ossie, for 17
years, Tony Costelloe for 15. 'We would work

Cream chiffon dress with purple
floral print, c. 1970.
Collection of Alfred Radley

together, [Ossie] would make up on the machine and then ask for help to put in a zip or sleeve if he couldn't manage it,' says Kathleen.

Celia worked at home on the print designs, without his input. Silk-screen-printing 10-yard lengths with an average of three colours, she would choose about 20 patterns a season. Some were calculated to go together, others would be put together by Ossie later. 'I'd test out the patterns on six very different fabrics,' she says, 'and then he would have the toile. What's interesting about his work is he'd start with his drawings and end with a finished garment; and you never see that nowadays because so few people can draw and make. He'd get the toile, draw what he wanted from that garment, and he'd take it off the mannequin, lay it flat and cut it. I don't think anyone knows how to do that any more, and that's what made them fit the body and made you feel nice because it was built around a 3-D form. That was brilliant for my prints because he'd often use two or three together, and they look good when you put different proportions together. That also worked very well. It was a formula.'

'We always started with a toile on a stand,' says Costelloe. 'The basic block of calico fitted on the stand. That bit was simple and then it became more complicated. One pattern was made of one piece of cardboard with two hooks, the dress made in one piece of chiffon, very ingenious – so complicated he had to

Celia's drawing of dress, red and black with a yellow stripe, skirt in yellow and black with swatch, muslin and jersey, c. 1970.

explain it to people. All of this was made in-house. He was an artist and brilliant technician. The chiffon dresses with Celia prints – a skirt might take four metres of fabric. He would cut on the straight and fit on the bias, which is more difficult to do, to get the drape perfect. We would pleat the fabric before cutting, fit godets into the skirts.'

Janey Ironside, quoted in an article in 1971, helped to explain Ossie's constant experimentation. [35] 'I used to be the Cassandra, pointing out that the mini could not be forever and that he ought to know about boned bodices and the like. So he learned. He is very creative still and his clothes are wearable, too. He can cut and prefers to do the cutting. I know. His clothes really work.' Both his cutter and machinist insist that he could cut every toile and prototype himself. It is important to understand this, given the rumour at the time that he employed a Dior-trained cutter who

was the real genius behind the name. When he told Georgina Howell years later in *The Sunday Times Magazine* that he was a 'master-cutter', [36] the hubris coloured a very real truth, a rare talent to design, cut and make original clothes that had the added power of unique and extraordinary prints.

'There were no great discussions about his work. He'd do little drawings,' says Kathleen. 'He was always drawing. Celia would do her designs first, then he would work out how it would be. Her drawings inspired him. His early things were in satin and silk.' In 1967, Ossie recorded that the Rolling Stones' Brian Jones, who lived at 52 Radnor Walk, and Keith Richards started wearing 'silks and satins printed by Celia and the skin-tight jewel-coloured trousers from a stash of pre-war corset satin A.P. found. I made men's shirts with frills in chiffon and in crêpe, with a one-sided collar, a leather jacket metallic with blue

*Ossie's watersnake-skin jacket
with zip, fitted at the waist,
'£28 13s 11d, Quorum
and Just Looking',
Vogue, 15 October 1968.*
Peccinotti © Vogue/
The Condé Nast Publications Ltd

snake. Marianne [Faithfull] bought a suede suit trimmed in python with a fluted peplum and never asked the price.'[37]

Tony Costelloe remembers the popularity of the snakeskins. They were exotic with the added glamour attached to wearing part of a dangerous animal and the association with fetish in clothing oneself in another creature's skin. And, of course, they were unisex, a big thing in the later 1960s. 'The revolutionary thing was using python skin, no one else had done that,' he says. 'The snakeskins would come in the full length from the warehouse. The watersnake was very glossy, in reds and greens, the python was much bigger and in a greeny-grey. We also did pearlized leather, also new. They were made up by Mr Kent in Streatham, a leather-maker.' One of the first was a leather jacket for Peter Hinwood, a model at English Boy and later to play Rocky in the film *The Rocky Horror Picture Show.*

The building at Radnor Walk was relatively new, dating to between the wars, and had been refurbished. The shop was on the ground floor, and there was a flat in the middle and a flat at the top, which was Ossie's workroom. The shop front had glass doors, and inside there were racks on either side and two single changing-rooms on the right. Ossie bought lots of different pieces of paper, which Celia describes as being a kind of camouflage, a 'cross between marble and animal skin', from a specialist shop in High Holborn,

pasted it on the walls and varnished it. The cubicles were in a pastel pink. Describing that time, she says: 'It was all beginning to emerge, with English Boy upstairs and David Gilmour [later of Pink Floyd] working as the van driver. I would go into Radnor Walk to be with the friends who hung out there.' Fiona Ronaldson describes this as a creative and gentle period, with Ossie in his studio drinking champagne and smoking dope, making clothes for socialites and rock stars. 'There was such freedom at the end of the 1960s and Ossie and Alice articulated this freedom through their clothes. We could walk down the road in see-through things with no fear of being attacked. For those who lived through this, it was an incredibly wonderful time.'

'Everyone would come to us,' remembers Tony Costelloe. 'Saturdays were very busy. 'Music would be all the current things played on a record player, the Stones, the Beatles, Family; the Isley Brothers, Black R&B. He and Alice were well connected socially but at the time we didn't think about it. All the wives and girlfriends would come in, Bianca, Bill Wyman's. Patti Boyd and Amanda Lear. Marianne Faithfull, Carina Frost. I loved Amanda. She lived an enchanted life, always a smiling face. They loved his flair and, looking back on it, he helped them too. We'd start the day at 9.00. He'd come in at 11.00 and say, "Right, we're going to make a dress for so-and-so to wear tonight." It would be an original Ossie, so he knew what they wanted. It was all very spontaneous.' Jenny Dearden, however, recalls that while the scene was egalitarian, looks and style were all-important. 'You had to look right. You had to be skinny. And you had to be pretty. But a lot of people there weren't fantastic-looking, but if they dressed in the right way…'

Patti Boyd, model and George Harrison's wife, first met Ossie at the shop. She describes

the attraction. 'The atmosphere was more residential than commercial. I would go to Quorum to see him. It was a good place to hang out with people that you knew; a small group, more bohemian than exclusive, but not necessarily elitist in the way that one means now. People who knew Ossie stood out. He was new and it was very difficult to find good clothes then. I would go antique markets like Chelsea Antiques Market because I liked antique fabrics and would make things myself in unique fabrics. Then I went to Quorum. Ossie was creating marvellous things, with great shapes, fluid around the hips. Whatever he designed seemed to suit my figure at the time and I loved the designs because they were so flattering. My favourite Ossie was a top, with slightly puffed sleeves, tight at the elbow and crossed at the front, tied at the back and pleated over the hips. You could wear a beautiful Ossie top with velvet trousers from Granny Takes a Trip. If he made something specially for you, he would name it after you, so there was a "Patti" dress.'

In 1967 Ossie moved in a new direction. He designed a romantic white jersey and organza collection, cut on the bias with full, soft frills around the arms. Transparent chiffon became a big feature, one of the strongest prints being flowers overprinted with trellis-like squares, with a longer, more flowing silhouette. Celia created a chiffon and georgette scarf collection, influenced by the artist Léon Bakst and the costumes he made for Nijinsky, Ossie's hero. Ossie also dropped his hemlines, potentially allowing for greater experimentation with the waist-to-neck area. An admirer of James Laver, who, in his *Taste and Fashion* (1937), had argued the theory of 'shifting erogenous zones' as an explanation of revelation and concealment in fashion history, Ossie realized that the hemline had reached its zenith and the

'I found the mini skirt restrictive. With the bias cut you could end up with the most extraordinary patterns...' Ossie Clark

bust would be the new area of interest.[38] 'Fashion has become a cliché,' he informed *Nova* in 1967. 'Everything is a variation on two shapes – short and waisted or short and straight. Long skirts mean designers have to re-think the top half. People will also start looking at the faces again instead of the legs.' He told the RCA students: 'When I did start to make clothes, the mini-skirt had become so ridiculously short that I noticed women, when they went to sit down, would make this movement holding on to their hem. I thought: "This is wrong," so I watched body language and I think that's where my success came from, anticipating what women wanted.'[39]

Candida Lycett Green describes what set him apart from his contemporaries. 'It was the clinging effect that was completely different from designers like Mary Quant and later, Bill Gibb, who did cardboard cut-out dresses that fitted on the body. Ossie made frocks from the body out. This was the dead opposite of Courrèges. Either you wanted to look like a fashion victim or you wanted to look seductive, in which case, you wore Ossie.' José Fonseca worked closely with him, as the English Boy offices were situated in the Radnor Walk building. Models included Amanda Lear, Suki Poitier, Chrissie Shrimpton, Kari-Ann Moller, Linda Keith and Marisa Berenson. 'We worked with Ossie a great deal. He loved women, loved to dress them and make them beautiful. He knew women's bodies and addressed them

when designing. What made him so special, in addition to this, was that he was a complete original, the fabrics were out of this world and he made people look fantastic. I can't think who does that today.'

The new skirt was based on traditional riding dress, creating what was immediately dubbed 'the midi'. It was a success; Dior had included it for Spring/Summer 1967 but the collection had flopped; both Ossie and Alice claimed to have done it first, however, and *Vogue* agreed, writing that Quorum was 'always six months ahead of everybody.'[40] Demonstrating that fashion so often reflects a contemporary mood, the film *Bonnie and Clyde*, released in 1967, was enormously popular and the 1920s costume with calf-length outfits had immediate impact, both in men's and women's fashion. Quorum, however, had sensed the mood, and beat their peers to the new retro spirit. 'People who are still staying, "Will it happen?" about the mid-calf length are off-beam. It has happened. His Spring range of long skirts and long culottes has been selling to stores for many weeks,' wrote *Nova*.[41]

Marit Allen remembers the effect of wearing Ossie-designed clothes at this time. 'He was magical. The clothes were intoxicating to wear. They made you feel omnipotent and feminine because they were so complimentary to the body. Not just lovely fabrics by Celia and good cutting: they were ethereal.' In 1968, four pages of *Vogue*'s March issue were devoted to the

YOUNG IDEA
THE WIZARD OF OSSIE

Ossie Clark is the wizard who designed the clothes on these four pages. He's a magician leading a magical mysterious change of fashion now. Translucent tulips blossoming on shimmering satin, opposite. Billowing sleeves growing into huge cuffs, a tall collar, a long blouse-belted tunic over flaring fluted trousers. Tunic, 7 gns, trousers, 5 gns. Print by Celia Birtwell. Lipstick, Barbara Gould's Ibis. Cigar by Benson & Hedges. A blouse for angels, below, waves of organdie rising from a deep neckline, over the shoulders to cascade down the sleeves. All bound with silk ribbon. 7 gns. Worn with a calf length black crepe skirt, 5 gns. All at Quorum, 52 Radnor Walk, S.W.3

new collection in 'The Wizard of Ossie,' photographed by David Bailey.[42] 'Putting together a fashion shoot with Ossie was enormous fun because Bailey had the energy. He enjoyed doing clothes because the clothes had energy too, and there wasn't a person in the room above 25,' she says. Her editorial conveys a sense of reverence in which the young designer was held. 'Ossie Clark is the wizard who designed the clothes on these four pages. He's a magician leading a magical mysterious change of fashion now. Translucent tulips blossoming on shimmering satin…Billowing sleeves growing into huge cuffs, a tall collar, a long blouse belted tunic over flaring fluted trousers…A blouse for angels, waves of organdie rising from a deep neckline, over the shoulders to cascade down the sleeves. All bound with silk ribbon…Worn with a calf-length black crêpe skirt…Looks like black magic. Black jersey jacket, with short tasselled sleeves, over a voluptuous V-necked satin shirt and mid-calf wool skirt…Black magic crêpe dress with a deep plunging neck and plunging sleeves and hem, plunging to mid-calf, all bound with slipper satin, with long silk tasselled on the waist tie.' Prices ranged from five to seven guineas.

This feature in *Vogue* set the seal on his success. He was soon to become, in the words of the press, 'the King of the King's Road' and dressmaker to the Beautiful People. Fiona Ronaldson, who had worked at *Vogue* before

previous pages
left
*Ossie wears one of his silk crêpe
shirts with a one-side collar and
one of his favourite Fair Isle
jumpers, knitted by his mother.
The belt is one that he made from
small pieces of leather.*
Portrait by Hans Feurer, c. 1968

right
*Ossie's sketch of ruffled chiffon
dress with tie neck, c. 1968–9.*

joining Quorum in 1970, says 'the press loved him. Alice never cared about publicity but Ossie did. He wanted to be a star. Quorum became the focus of the old aristocracy and the new aristocracy of the time. It was part of the radical, artistic subculture.'

On 7 August 1968, riding high on its success, with Twiggy, Brigitte Bardot and Britt Ekland numbering among its customers, Quorum unveiled its 'Nude Look' collection, transparent chiffon tops which were open at the front and not meant to be worn with a bra. 'Not content with just see-throughs…they've added new spice with open-hanging jacket-and-pants suits worn with no bra,' reported the *International Herald Tribune.* 'Even when jackets or kimonos are belted, they open in a wide vee to the bellybutton. Many trouser suits are made in very filmy printed chiffon or clinging

satin, worn over nothing but a birthday suit.' [43] It also wrote that Ossie had been nominated for the British Export Council fashion award and that Macy's had invited him to New York as a distinguished guest. Confounding those who may have thought the romantic chiffon style was to be his only contribution to fashion, he designed the 'Lamborghini' suit, a long, closely fitted satin jacket with numerous buttons as a detail and a high round-tipped collar, with Celia-print satin trousers. All the clothes were given names; 'Flopsy', 'Mopsy' and 'Cottontail'; 'Acapulco Gold'; 'Bridget'; 'Cuddly'; 'Ouidjeta Banana'; 'Lily'; 'Celia'; 'Ophelia' and 'Bianca'.
'It was a fun and creative thing to do,' explains Adie Hunter.

In autumn 1968, his ankle-length 'maxi' collection appeared. *Vogue* featured model

4 for Vogue.
6 Dec.

*Ossie's drawing of a flared trouser
suit with floral pattern, c. 1968–9.
'Everyone wanted that early
look that was really the look for
the night,' Jenny Dearden.*

Maudie James wearing a streamlined tweed
coat inspired by the 1790s redingote, complete
with the cane popular with the fashionable
'Amazons' of the period, in a photograph by
David Montgomery. 'If you look like this, you
must be responsible for another revolution,'
it cautioned. [44]

Beatrix Miller, *Vogue*'s editor-in-chief, greatly
admired him. 'His cut was brilliant, his evening
dresses a source of sensual and romantic images
in *Vogue*. I think some of his most memorable
work was inspired by Celia Birtwell's magical
textile designs in satin and chiffon. He was a
notable player at a high point in the blossoming
of young and innovative British fashion.'

Adie Hunter comments on how Ossie's
ideal sometimes differed from that of the more
conventional *Vogue*: it saw beautiful, floating

right

*Ossie's soft-pink Harris tweed
maxi coat, inspired by
the 1790s redingote,*
Vogue, 15 October 1968.
*Tony Costelloe: 'That was
when he started doing
those high collars.'*
**David Montgomery © Vogue/
The Condé Nast Publications Ltd**

opposite

*Ossie's yellow crêpe trousers
and chiffon top, c. 1971.*
**V&A: T. 301 & A-1985.
Given by Mr Paul Getty**

fantasies, while he was striving towards combining this with a more tailored structure. 'Bea Miller, the editor at *Vogue*, adored him. Grace Coddington appreciated him, but he wasn't really in her realm; her hair would be scraped back and she'd wear these little outfits; very un-Ossie. Sometimes he didn't really like the way *Vogue* did it. They'd put clothes with Maudie James and create a romantic, floating, Sarah Moon-look. He really made clothes with girls like Gala Mitchell in his mind, a woman with breasts, a small waist and slim hips.' The photographer Barry Lategan shot Ossie's work for *Vogue* and remembers the exciting possibilities of the chiffons. 'Ossie had a strong sense of tailoring. There were frills and soft fabrics but a lot of tailoring. It was very helpful shooting chiffons because one could blow the clothes with a machine. Up until then, pictures had been static. With chiffons we could show more of the sense of the ephemeral.' With hindsight, Brian Godbold described how the chiffons suggested a talent that went beyond that of most British fashion designers. 'The wispy chiffon dresses were magical at that point. Because of the Hockney connection, he felt he was an artist. We were all aware at the time that he was extremely talented. With Ossie, it was very much about a feeling for fabric. His craftsmanship was superb, and his cut was very creative.'

Between 1968 and 1974 there were two distinct Ossie Clark styles: floating chiffons

'I would present my collection of fabrics on his table in the studio and he would start making extraordinary clothes. And usually the better ones came at the very end, like a day before the show. His best work would emerge towards a deadline.' Celia Birtwell

opposite

Ossie's 'Nude Look' with satin trousers gathered at the knee, inspired by Diaghilev, both in Celia prints, chosen by Prudence Glynn, fashion editor of The Times *as her 'Dress of the Year' for the Museum of Costume in Bath.*

The Museum of Costume, Bath

with prints by Celia, close-fitting round the arms and bust, and tailored clothes in tweeds, satin, leather and crêpe, in plain colours or with Celia designs printed and embroidered on them. Leslie Poole believes that 'he liberated women by constructing the low neckline with a bib front, tied at the back. It could fit anybody. It had gathers but no darts to point at the bust, so it was very different from Dior and Chanel in look. It was much freer, it suited the freedom of the age, with clothes that were sexy and loose, and that's what he gave to fashion. The light, sexy tie-on dress was really based on a 1940s washing dress, and he may have seen his mother wearing one. He borrowed lots of things from old film-star books, like pointy sleeves and bias cut, but he effectively altered fashion through this new construction. He paved the way for other young designers; certainly Zandra Rhodes.'

Collections were presented to an adoring audience twice a year. 'He brought showbiz to fashion,' says Norman Bain. 'These were the first fashion shows that were like happenings, pop concerts and theatre. The feeling was that of a Parisian salon; everybody was there together, writers, artists, actors, dancers.' The show at the Revolution Club, just behind Berkeley Square in Mayfair, in 1968, saw Jimi Hendrix and the Rolling Stones in the audience. Patti Boyd, who only did runway shows for Quorum, wore a cream chiffon dress with a print of blue birds and irritated her husband, George Harrison, in the audience with the rest of the Beatles, by going bra-less. Cynthia Lennon was there too. Jane Ormsby Gore remembers 'I took my son Saffron along with me. People didn't look very interesting in those days. It was all very new. And Ossie was just extraordinary. His clothes were better cut than his contemporaries' because he understood women's shapes.'

In 1969, further official recognition of his role in fashion was given by Prudence Glynn, fashion editor for *The Times*, who chose the 'Nude Look' Ossie chiffon top and satin trousers with prints by Celia as the 'Dress of the Year' for the Museum of Costume in Bath. 'This chiffon tunic dress with its matching satin pants from Ossie Clark exemplifies the 1969 look at its most appealing and its most subtle,' she wrote. 'Above and beyond the essential qualities which I have already listed, it has complete originality and a sympathy of taste which women have a right to expect from a dress designer. Ossie Clark is, I believe, in the world class for talent; in fact I think that we should build a completely modern idea of British high fashion around him. We should stop being amazed by our creative talent and start capitalizing on it, as do the French and the Italians…'[45]

'The King of the King's Road'

Prudence Glynn's plea to the British fashion industry to start capitalizing on British talent was made soon after Quorum had sold its business to a London wholesaler. Despite being the most fashionable of London boutiques, it was broke, with debts of £70,000. In June 1968, its book-keeper had approached the British manufacturing company Radley Fashions in Eastcastle Street, off Oxford Street, in the heart of the British 'rag-trade' district. Radley had just become a public company, selling its collections to boutiques and department stores at an average of 1,000 a week – 50,000 garments a year. It produced collections that were at the top end of the market and employed, over the years, Betty Jackson, Sheridan Barnett, Rosie Bradford and Wendy Dagworthy as in-house designers.

Al Radley first discussed the deal with Alice Pollock. It seemed like a dream ticket: the mass market coming together with two leading designers, a new shop as a showcase for Quorum, and Ossie now to be given enough financial support to allow him to develop as a designer. Radley bought Whitelight Clothiers, a company owned by Alice and Ossie operating the Quorum boutique, and the two companies that ran Quorum, Alice Pollock Limited and Ossie Clark (London) Limited. Alice was to retain 25 per cent and Ossie was to receive a salary and a royalty based on sales. Celia was to design for Alice, Ossie and for the new wholesale line. Ossie was to continue with his couture, with the top range 'Ossie Clark for Quorum', and design the wholesale 'Ossie Clark for Radley.' Workrooms and a new studio were opened at nearby 6 Burnsall Street. It was a financial coup for Ossie. Felicity Green reported in the *Daily Mirror* that the first Radley collection 'has sold "like a bomb", [Radley] admits, with happily raised eyebrows. As one perhaps slightly over-enthusiastic store buyer

'What made him special was that he was completely original, the fabrics were out of this world and he made people look fantastic.' José Fonseca

put it, "He's real fashion. He's one of the few originals. He's a genius!"' [46]

'Within two or three years Ossie was earning £23,000, bought a Bentley, a house and travelled all over the world,' says Radley. The new shop was an old fishmonger's, 113 King's Road. Alice had ideas for the shop that were far-seeing and Al Radley now regrets not listening to her and following them through. She wanted it to be a place with a coffee shop and sofas, where people could come and read newspapers or books, make themselves at home, peruse the clothes at their leisure. This idea of a relaxed lifestyle emporium was realized on a grand scale by Biba at their new shop in the old Derry and Tom's building in Kensington High Street. Instead, the new Quorum, which opened in spring 1969, was to be a state-of-the-art boutique with 'Quorum' in neon letters, dark-brown plate glass windows at the front and a central revolving steel door. Another, smaller

right

Ossie sits between Alice Pollock (on his right) and Chelita Secunda at the Quorum Charity Christmas party in aid of Save the Children Fund, at the Royal Albert Hall, 9 December 1968. Chelita wears an Ossie python-skin trouser suit; staff would be paid a salary and be given an outfit per week.

opposite

Twiggy's python-skin coat, trimmed and lined with arctic fox, that Ossie made for her American tour in 1969.
© **Warrington Museum and Art Gallery**

shop was opened in Hampstead in 1972, managed by Fiona Ronaldson: 'By then Mr Radley decided to be more "hands-on" and would sometimes come and sit in the shop on Saturdays, watching how business was going.'

The King's Road shop had two floors with fake wood panelling on the walls, a black Pirelli rubber floor, and eight changing-rooms to allow for the steady flow of new customers who could buy an 'Ossie Clark for Radley' for under £20, instead of the top range priced at anything up to £300, the sum singer Eartha Kitt had paid for Ossie's python-skin dress in 1968. In addition there was a small menswear range and knitwear, jewellery by Ken Lane, scarves by Celia, Italian enamel rings, American and French belts and tights. Shop-lifting was a problem, as was industrial espionage, according to Tony Costelloe: 'People would steal things. They could roll the chiffons into little balls

and stuff them in their knickers or put a jacket on underneath their coat and walk out of the shop. Once we had a guy who was sitting in the shop for about a week. He would ask about the clothes. We thought he was one of the girls' boyfriends, but we got a call saying that he was a paid spy getting information on the range at Quorum.'

The shop didn't have the intimate feeling of Radnor Walk, however, where friends would sit and drink with Ossie in the staff room at the back, or join him in his studio. 'It had all been so free and easy before,' says Fiona Ronaldson. 'A Managing Director called Brian Shack was appointed in 1972. Ossie and Alice hated him. The first thing he did was put a padlock on the storeroom door.' Nevertheless, Radnor Walk had been intimidating for some. 'I didn't like going there because the Chelsea Set would be ensconced,' says Norman Bain. 'Some of the shop assistants could be very superior, too.'

right
*Cream silk chiffon blouse with
a combination of designs,
pussy-cat bow at the neck and
layered sleeves, c. 1969.*
© **Warrington Museum
and Art Gallery**

opposite
*Ossie's romantic white chiffon
dress with Celia's black and green
clover-leaf design is worn by model
Helga James, the skirt and cuffs
with handkerchief points.
The old-fashioned covered buttons
with handmade loops were typical
of Ossie. This fashion shoot by
Norman Parkinson is set on
the shores of Lake Tana in
Ethiopia, at sunset.
The young boy in the boat
wears Ethiopa's national dress,
the* shamma, *in fine white cotton.*
Vogue, *January 1969.*
**Norman Parkinson Ltd/
Fiona Cowan**

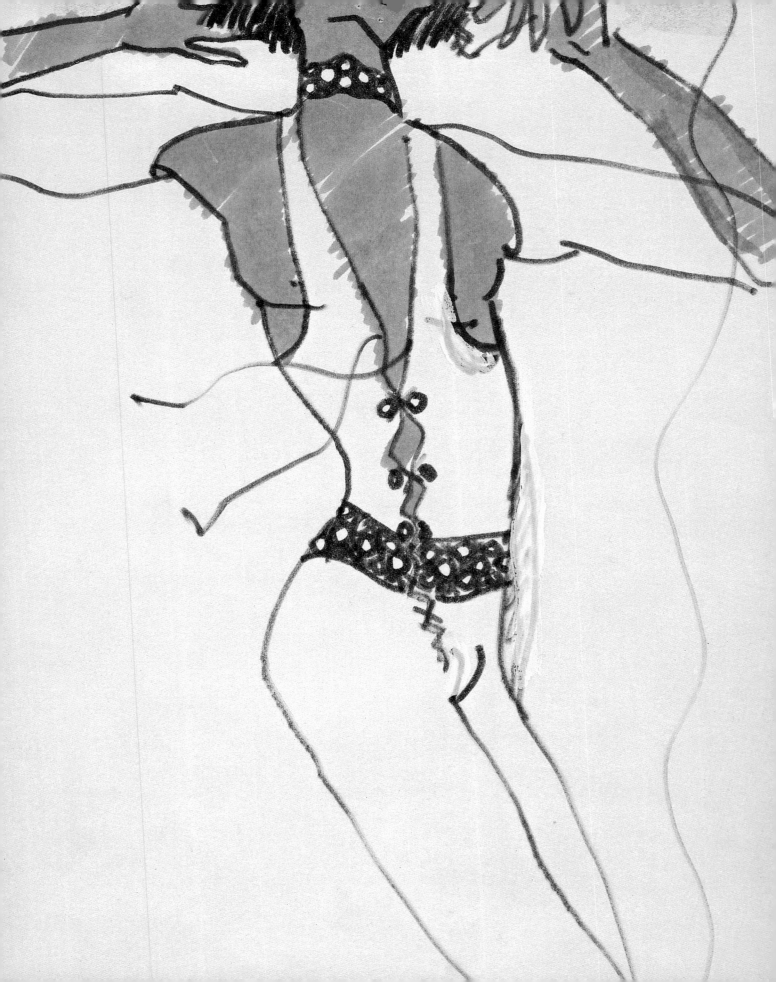

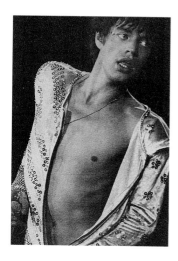

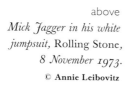

opposite and above right
*Ossie's designs for Mick Jagger's
white jumpsuit, 1973.
'Mick had a vision in his
head of what he wanted to be
and Ossie implemented that
vision.' The jumpsuits would
be unzipped on stage.
Adie Hunter: 'I remember
Ossie fitting Mick's suits in
Burnsall Street, Jagger with
his little jackets and tiny hips.
He approached designing for
men and women in the same way,
and Jagger had the same
femininity as Ossie.'*

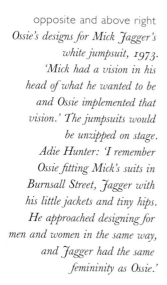

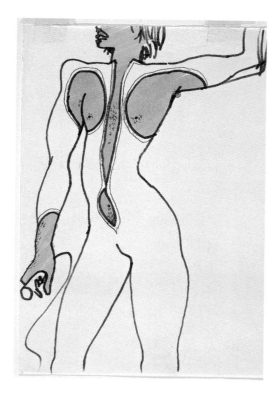

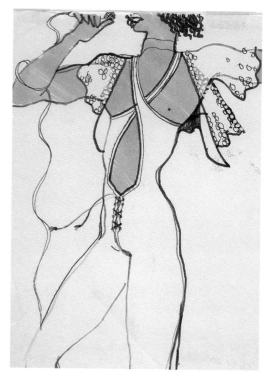

Frances Ronaldson remembers: 'The Rolling Stones and Marianne Faithfull, all those people were coming into Quorum all the time. It was like a party down there actually, smoking dope, drinking wine, chatting away, having a good time, and Ossie was cutting clothes and stitching them in the background.'

Ossie had first made clothes for Mick Jagger in 1968, when he was taken into Quorum by Marianne Faithfull. 'We made things for him,' recalls Tony Costelloe, 'a jumpsuit in leather. Ossie would have to put him in it, it was so complicated, ties with laces. For the 1972 tour we made a blue velvet fabric all-in-one suit, stapled with hundreds of silver circles so they glittered on stage. We had to make four or five for the tour because they didn't last long.' Frances Ronaldson remembers a gold leather jumpsuit that Jagger was to wear for a concert at Earls Court in 1973. 'He looked like a prancing lion. Alice and Ossie had some faithful Spanish

seamstresses that used to work with them. They did lots of stuff themselves. Alice would go berserk on the print table. And I was saying, "Yes, we can do this and then we can do that next." And Alice would get completely spaced out in the end, high on the idea of printing, wanting to change everything halfway through the print run. And we always did very short lengths because they were just the samples – it's terribly uneconomical to work like that. It was about producing fabulous things if you possibly could, but not really thinking about the future.'

Nicky Samuel, then married to Nigel Waymouth, owner of Granny Takes a Trip, met Ossie in 1970. She was one of his greatest customers, able to afford his couture dresses, as well as ready-to-wear Quorum and Ossie Clark for Radley. He made her a dress embroidered with moons and stars, with a leather halter-neck. 'He wanted to make clothes for me; I had a big bust and tiny hips and the bias cuts looked

wonderful. Another was a wonderful cream silk skirt cut like a tulip. He knew how to make one look extremely good. The evening dresses, including the chiffons, were cut tight around the shoulders and armholes and one was still in a period when one was prepared to be slightly uncomfortable – sometimes one didn't breathe in too deeply – but the chiffon day dresses were comfortable. One could wear them with or without underwear, often teamed up with a satin jacket.' The secret pocket in an Ossie dress, which has gone down in legend, was reserved only for specially made dresses.

By now, the Quorum fashion shows had become major events at which a broad variety of London personalities met in a kind of chic melting-pot. Ossie would make tapes and Tony Howard, who worked with Pink Floyd, produced the music. To celebrate the opening of the shop there was a fashion show at Chelsea Town Hall, presenting Alice and Ossie's boutique collections. Ossie only noted that Gala Mitchell, his favourite model took part, John Lennon and Yoko Ono sent a good luck note and that he received 30 bouquets of flowers.

Adie Hunter took over Quorum's PR from Chelita Secunda shortly after this. There was work for her to do. 'I was much more grounded and always encouraged him while bringing him

right
Ossie fitting Gala, his favourite
model, in Burnsall Street.
They met in 1963; she was
'bored in a mink coat'.

opposite
The sun and moon dress
that Ossie made for Nicky Samuel,
satin-backed silk crêpe with
embroidery and appliqué, c. 1971.
She and Ossie were close friends.
He loved nature, astrology
and the night sky, particulary
the moon. This is literally
a 'magic' dress.
© **Warrington Museum**
and Art Gallery

down to earth,' she says. 'He'd be enthusiastic about something like a tree because he found nature exciting, and he loved women, stylish women, women who had something. Ernestine Carter, fashion editor of *The Sunday Times,* was encouraged to visit, as was Alison Adburghman of the *Guardian,* and the coverage in both newspapers was expanded; the former sent along Michael Roberts to draw a collection. Suzy Menkes and Prudence Glynn continued to support him, understanding the important influence of couture in his work.

One of the first practical things Adie did was to organize a press book for Ossie and for Radley, which no one had done before, and she attended fashion shoots. This proved invaluable in that it allowed her some control over the presentation of the Quorum image. 'No-one knew how to tie the chiffons. I remember Bailey photographing Marie. I had to help tie the dress at the neck because it was complicated.'

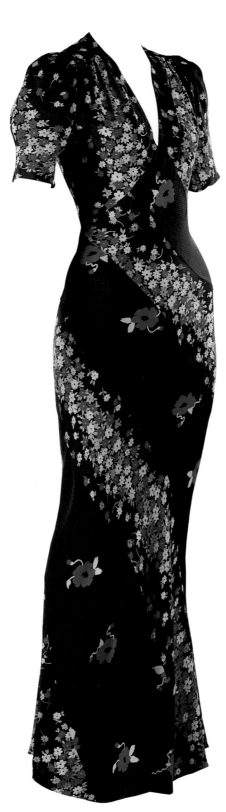

Bias-cut viscose crêpe-de-Chine dress with red and yellow floral 'discharge' print by Celia, c. 1974.
Collection of Alfred Radley

'He had a new take on femininity. He emphasized the bust with ties around the waist and with the flowing skirts, it was totally new.' Edina Ronay

Adie remembers watching Ossie work. 'He could start from the very beginning of a garment and handsew it himself. I found it fascinating and very inspirational.' His cutting of the Daisy Whirligig dress, in embroidered marocain crêpe, made a particular impression. 'Suddenly one night he cut out a circular pattern on the floor and it was just incredible. I thought, "How can this possibly be a dress?" It was amazing, completely on the bias. It just looked like a helter-skelter thing – this great long piece of brown paper. When it was made, it was incredible because, being in marocain and the way it was cut, it was like elastic. It took the shape of anybody. At the time, everybody wanted to wear Ossie so Radley did certain dresses a few seasons later.'

The venue for the spring 1970 Quorum show was again Chelsea Town Hall on the King's Road. Music was by Steve Miller and the Juicy Hot Rats, Leonard styled the 'wild hair

for the models, getting wilder as they danced, sparkling greeny eye make-up, carmine lips and clothes in a garden of colours,' reported *Vogue.*[47] Amanda Lear, Patti Boyd, Kari-Ann Moller (later Jagger) and Gala Mitchell were among the models making it a sensation, and present in the audience were Janey Ironside and Lady Diana Cooper, wearing an Ossie ensemble, a black jersey dress with a snakeskin biker jacket over her shoulders, with Cecil Beaton.

Frances Ronaldson, who had just joined Quorum to work as textile designer to Alice Pollock, was backstage at the shows with the Quorum team. 'They were wild and wonderful events. I would push the models on because they were all spaced out. We had some of the girls who worked with Andy Warhol and one was doing the can-can with no knickers on in a wonderful dress and wouldn't get off the stage. I had to push her off. The models were absolutely fantastic. Alice always picked out

these marvellous black girls she saw in the streets like Kellie and Agnes.'

In 1970, Ossie and Celia joined Penelope Tree, Mick Jagger, Jean Shrimpton, Rudolf Nureyev, Dr Roy Strong, Patrick Procktor, Lord David Cecil and others at Cecil Beaton's Wiltshire home, Reddish House, to be filmed by David Bailey for a television programme he was making for the ATV channel. 'It was a mixture of people all looking interesting in their new autumn clothes. Many looked beautiful,' Beaton told the magazine, for its story, 'Double Take',[48] which showed Penelope Tree wearing a black panne velvet suit by Ossie, holding the mysterious Mexican Datura lily in her left hand. This was a sybaritic scene, and Ossie regarded himself as an artist, occupying a bohemian world rather than committing himself totally to the business of fashion.

Full of talent, a lack of discipline was becoming apparent. He and Celia married in

1969 and their son Albert was born in October that year. Despite this stability, his own lifestyle was increasingly dominated by intense work and, in reaction, intense partying, with the attendant popular drugs of the time. 'When he was on a roll,' says Adie Hunter, 'before a show, he was churning out ideas. When the show was over, he wasn't interested. That's where Alice was good. She could look at his work, see what would sell and select. She did it without compromising it.'

Alice described her philosophy behind the Quorum environment, which now numbered 30 people. 'It's not just work: it's an ideal…I really believe in opportunity. I've always been lucky myself and I want to create opportunities for others. It is more difficult now because there's so much at stake. But I'm careful about whom I employ. I wouldn't have anyone here I wouldn't like to live with. It's absolutely free here…I design separates, Celia Birtwell does prints and Ossie does dresses. He has incredible technical knowledge plus enormous original talent. He can make one perfect garment and a pattern for 200 more. That's very important. So many people have lovely ideas but can't execute them.' [49] Ossie's bias-cut chiffons and moss crêpes were increasingly popular, and he was always developing his technique, seeing how fabrics of different weights and textures responded: 'There's a limitation with the bias cut and it works better on a woman with broader shoulders and narrower hips and less bosom. It's not easy to wear. At the time it was a statement, a rejection of all that had gone before really. When you start experimenting with the bias cut and you look at people who are famous for it – Madame Vionnet and Charles James and the like – you find there are certain problems and when you come to them, you can look at their work and you can see that they didn't overcome those problems either.' [50]

above
*Kari-Ann Jagger.
Ossie's business card, c. 1975.*

opposite
*Celia's drawing of red and green
culottes and bias-cut floor-length
dress, c. 1969.*

Vanessa de Lisle, who had worked in fashion in Italy, returned to London with one ambition: to work for Ossie Clark. She joined Quorum, working in the shop, but was soon snapped up by Adie Hunter, becoming her assistant. She conveys a sense of the atmosphere: 'All I wanted was a job with Ossie because I knew it was extraordinary. Every morning we had to check the stock in the shop because people kept stealing the clothes. Ossie didn't have people around him that he didn't like; he would have got rid of someone in his quiet way. There was an old-fashioned tea-lady called Doris, so it was very down to earth. You had to fit in and not be a groupie. The stars would come in and out of the shop – Mick Jagger, David Hockney, Amanda Lear, Patti Boyd, Marianne Faithfull. Nobody was impressed, we just carried on working. No-one rang up the press when someone famous came in.' His studio in Burnsall Street was a light, clean, quiet space, where he worked with Tony Costelloe, Kathleen Coleman and the other studio staff. She describes his dexterity: '[Ossie's] hands were like a pianist's, long fingers that turned up at the ends. He would drape and cut everything on a mannequin, Tony and he never stopping pinning and writing things down. The mannequin was based on Kari-Ann's body and she would come in endlessly for fittings. I would think, "How can this man create this fantasticness every season?" Every dress was perfect.'

In 1970, Lady Rendlesham, director of the Rive Gauche shop in New Bond Street, spoke to Didier Grumbach, owner of the French manufacturer Mendes, about working with British designers. 'I just thought it would be nice for a designer to go across the Channel and have his clothes made up the way they are made up in France,' she told the *Evening Standard*.[51] Mendes produced the Saint Laurent

above
*Ossie's show for Mendes at the
Louvre, 22 April 1971.
'Ossie Clark's collection was
a fantasy of the finest silks…
Audacious and incredibly
feminine,' wrote Marit Allen
in* Vogue, *June 1971.*
© **Vogue/The Condé Nast
Publications Ltd**

opposite
*Ossie sketch of two outfits,
c. 1970.*

Rive Gauche collection and ready-to-wear for Courrèges, Givenchy and Ungaro. Grumbach approached Ossie and Jean Muir, proposing that they design *prêt-à-porter* collections, which would be distributed in France and the US by his company. Ossie agreed. He spent two months in Paris choosing fabrics and working with Mendes, which allowed him the kind of freedom and scope that would have been impossible in London. He loved the experience, calling his Paris cutter 'The Queen of the Drape'. 'You know, she put every pin in the same direction. At an angle of 45 degrees. Wow!'[52]

Percy Savage, a close friend of both Claire Rendlesham and Ossie and a consultant at Mendes, explains what this must have meant to the young designer. 'He was the Fath or Givenchy of London, with a high understanding of good workmanship. He had a real respect for couture and was making clothes to a higher standard than the British couture houses at the

time.' But Ossie had allowed his antipathy to French designers to grow ever since his days at the RCA, when he fell in love with Hollywood's costume designs. 'Bernard Nevill showed us that Paris wasn't the be-all-and-end-all of clothing. The rag-trade in England was run by this mentality of always assuming that the French knew best and the only way to make a statement was to copy what the French did.'[53] Ever since he had started at Quorum, he had felt that British fashion talent was regarded as secondary to that of the French. He had purposefully moved to create an aesthetic that was all his own, but saw that the British fashion industry did not support its designers in a way that compared with the French. Alice Pollock, as ever, was supportive, telling *The Sunday Times* that Quorum was his home, but it simply didn't have the workroom facilities or workmanship of an equivalent French fashion house. 'They have been copying Ossie for ages. Now he'll be

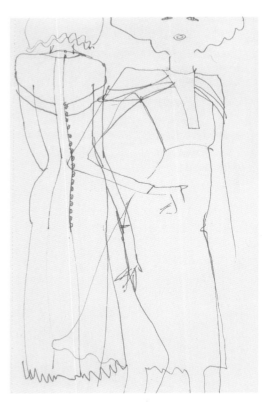

left
Ossie's drawing of a dress
with a halter neck, which placed
the focus on the shoulders,
similar to his voluptuous knitwear
designs, c. 1970.

right
Ossie's drawing of long
buttoned dress, c. 1970.

opposite
Ossie's drawing of a
day dress with yoke and
back detail, c. 1970.

doing it himself.'[54] There was a touch of the traditional English John Bull in the way both he and the press dealt with the Mendes invitation. 'Now he's in couture, as well as ready-to-wear, he'll put the skids under the French. Ossie is in the same class as Yves Saint Laurent. In time, he'll be better,' declared Jeffrey Wallis of the Wallis Shop group in 1971.[55] Instead of approaching the project with quiet intelligence, Ossie was unwisely arrogant: 'I wanted to show the French where fashion is these days. I think I made my point.'[56]

In April 1971, he presented his Paris collection for autumn. It was, in the words of the *Guardian*, 'restrained',[57] again 1940s-inspired, beautifully tailored and controlled. Reporting on the 22 April show at the Louvre, Marit Allen wrote in *Vogue*: 'Ossie Clark's collection was a fantasy of the finest silks, cut velvet and dotted chiffon, cut into parachute frills and knife-edge pleats, plunging necks and clinging insets. A satin guitar set as a stomacher into plum crêpe was his favourite – incredibly contoured seams across the back, with knife pleats springing from jacket insets, long skirts alive with cut, flare and frills, pleats and peplums; and his ultimate raincoat, cut flared from riding mac fabric – long puffed sleeves, huge collar. Audacious and incredibly feminine. The French were amazed and amused by the crazy glamour of Gala Mitchell, Ossie's London girl.'[58]

The show was a success, but instead of consolidating his position, Ossie repeated his pattern of following intense work with what was effectively a collapse. He produced only one collection for Mendes, and the contract ended after this. Kathleen Coleman loyally believes that the arrangement with Mendes did not continue because it was made virtually impossible for Ossie to carry on with it. Al Radley refutes this. Appointments were made with the French manufacturers that Ossie did

not keep. But Percy Savage believes: 'If Ossie had had the right money and backers, he could have done a better job than Saint Laurent. It was getting the collection from Ossie that was the problem.'

A new collection was presented in London at the Royal Court Theatre on 25 May 1971. It was one of the most sensational Quorum events. The Art Deco-style invitation featured an Ossie pin-up in Betty Grable pose and stated 12 midnight as starting time. In fact, it did not begin until 2.30. It was sponsored by the makers of Black Magic chocolates and the textile manufacturer Courtaulds, and there was a box of chocolates was on every seat, since Ossie loved their Art Deco design. Unfortunately, when the boxes were opened they revealed seasonal Easter eggs and bunnies, not the special chocolates he had wanted as the final, elegant touch to the event. He was absolutely furious. Norman Bain had arrived early for the event. 'Every one was stick-thin, so

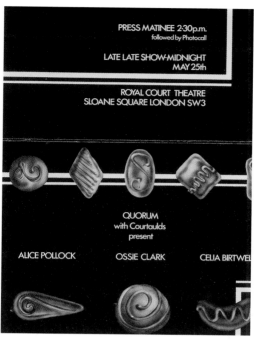

no-one ate the chocolates apart from me. I had a
very good seat, and just before the show started,
Linda McCartney, dressed in blue, with blue
hair, too, and Paul sat down beside me. There
was a furious flashing of camera lights; the A-
list audience was as much of a part of the show
as the clothes. Towards the back of the stage
there was a gauze curtain, the kind used in a
theatre. As the lights in the auditorium went
down, the lights behind the curtain were put on,
and we could see Ossie framed behind it,
cigarette in hand, dressing each of the models.
It was part of the performance, putting each
garment back on to a hanger and helping them
into something else. So the whole thing was
much slower and the models, who were out of
their heads, were as always allowed to do it all
in their own time. The music was of the
moment, the newest thing that people were
listening to, the thing that was out that week. It
was that immediate.' The event took about two

hours and was an intense visual and aural
experience. 'There was always incredible music
for the Quorum shows,' recalls Frances
Ronaldson. 'A lot of black music and R&B, Lou
Reed too, "Walk on the Wild Side" was always
played, with the black models, who not many
other designers worked with at the time. "Power
to the People" was Ossie's favourite and
everyone would sing along.'

For her *Evening Standard* page, Suzy Menkes
wrote: 'With a cast of famous names off stage
and on, Ossie Clark staged the fashion
spectacular of the year in Chelsea last night.
They flocked to the Royal Court Theatre at
midnight – Penelope Tree in a see-through
chiffon blouse, her companion, David Bailey,
in a shimmering liquorice-black suit. Outside
on the steps, the pop world fought to get inside.
Restaurateur Michael Chow in a cerise satin
blazer headed a contingent of Oriental trendies.

'Lord Harlech, whose daughter Alice

Nicky Samuel in transparent red chiffon dress, c. 1972.

Ormsby-Gore was modelling in the show, stood with his wife at the side of the packed auditorium searching for a seat, while blond painter David Hockney fell asleep in his seat of honour in the front row. On stage, the models gyrated across the flowery set in Ossie's latest figure-hugging dresses. Shoulders, cleavages and nipples were all revealed in the slashed-away shapes, boldly printed in scarlet and black. Patti Boyd twirled around in a cape-topped dress that showed her naked breasts beneath. Carina Fitzalan-Howard and henna-haired Gala slid on in ruched tarts' dresses, their platform-soled shoes glittering with sequins. And when actress Patti d'Arbanville pulled her midi-skirt up past her thighs, she had an appreciative audience in the tiny Chelsea theatre shouting and whistling for more.' [59] Kari-Ann Jagger, who had taken part in the Youthquake tours showcasing young British fashion abroad, argues that Ossie changed the idea of a runway show. 'Ossie went one step further. The music was incredible and we were allowed to do our own thing. Before that, we'd just walk up and down. There were queues outside the building trying to get in, the audience was full of beautiful people.' [60] Artist Andrew Logan says in admiration, 'Those women who modelled, Gala, Kari-Ann, Patti, Carina, they were such amazing, powerful people too. Ossie's shows were the start of everything we see today.' [61] Included in the show were 'Cameo lily', a printed dress with deep décolleté and front pleats, £25; 'Snowflake', a printed marocain with a halter neck and jacket, £17, 'Fans', a printed marocain dress with all-round pleated skirt, around £31, 'Pineapple', in marocain with black suede inset, £26.50; 'Moon and Stars', in black crêpe satin with red embroidery and suede inset on the bodice and nine yards of pleats in the skirt, £85; and 'Gypsy Girl Suit', in printed marocain, £23.50.

Ossie and friends celebrating after the Mallord Street show, 1972.

following page
Ossie cross-legged on a bed, Mo McDermott's tree sculpture on a shelf and a white telephone on the floor (very fashionable), echoing the one in the Hockney double portrait, c. 1970.
Johnny Dewe Matthews

Manolo Blahnik, who had arrived in London in 1970, was asked to design the shoes for the 1972 show and others that followed. For this one, again at the Royal Court Theatre, he created shoes with ivy leaves twined around the leg and decorated with cherries. [62] 'The women were like vamps. Kari-Ann, Amanda, Kellie, Gala and Penelope Tree acting to a point of overacting. It was an incredible vision,' he says. 'It was a frisson for everybody, everything was new and I have never seen anything like it since. He created an incredible magic with the body, he transported people out of reality and achieved what fashion should do – produce desire.'

Despite this phenomenon, all had not been well on the business side for some time. Rumours that the King's Road shop and model agency Monty's were to close had proved to be true, [63] and the Quorum shop had moved back to Radnor Walk. Celia was said to be against the decision; Ossie was not available for

comment. As Al Radley explained, the problem was that other shops in the King's Road, such as Just Looking, were selling 'Ossie Clark for Radley' and undermining Quorum, which simply did not have enough variety of stock on the rails to bring in the public. 'The boutique is affecting the wholesale side, which has gone up so rapidly. The idea of the shop was to launch the Ossie Clark name. Now all the shops down the King's Road want the Ossie stuff and if you can buy it in six other places, the shop has outlived its purpose.' [64]

The wholesale line by Radley was selling in Germany, Italy, Switzerland and the US, and they had their own concession in Harrods, but, says Vanessa de Lisle, 'the business side was not good. Not enough money was coming in to support Quorum.' Radley's system was to take Ossie's drawings and adapt them with the help of designer Rosie Bradford. These would be passed by Ossie and produced as the wholesale

ranges of dresses, separates and knitwear twice a year. These were very popular, such as the 'Cuddly' dress and 'Floating Daisy' dress, with its Celia print top and plain long skirt in moss crêpe that sold 20,000 copies. 'I regret not being firmer with him and employing a team of designers working in a studio producing under his name, just as happens in Paris,' he says. 'Ossie was very difficult; he wouldn't even talk to the other designers that worked for me.' Nor would he let Celia design for Alice, cracking down when she would use leftover fabric from his collections. This was a sensible decision given that their creative collaboration was an essential part of his work and the success of Quorum, but it led to increasing acrimony.

Celia by now was working with Courtaulds, extending her work to designing woven and embroidered as well as printed fabrics. In the last few weeks of her first pregnancy, she had produced 12 new designs for fabrics. 'Sometimes I am torn between the child and the work. But I know I must work so that Ossie can go on with his next collection. It's frightening to have this responsibility for Ossie. But I inspire Ossie and he inspires me. Since I was five I have been drawing fantasy fashion. The thing is that Ossie makes the fantasy work. I think of the arrangement as pattern on the body.' David Hockney immortalized this relationship in his double portrait, *Mr and Mrs Clark and Percy*, wittily dubbed 'Bottichelsea style' by pundits, which he painted in 1970–1. In fact, Percy was Blanche the cat. Celia, who was pregnant with their second son, George, is wearing Ossie's black moss crêpe wrap-around dress with spiral sleeves in red and black, designed in 1969.

'The painting of Ossie and Celia took about six months to do because I was painting it at [the studio in] Powis Terrace, sometimes they would come and pose there, although it was set in Linden Gardens,' says the artist, who also worked from photographs of the scene. 'I had done some double portraits before but in a way, I was painting people very close to me, the idea at the time was to make a portrait when not many people were doing them. In the picture I reversed things, with the lady standing and the man sitting down – it is a reversal of a classic 18th-century portrait.' It was not his first picture of either of them; his first drawing of Ossie, in blue pencil, dates back to the RCA days and Celia was to become a muse for Hockney. Celia, of course, had also been Ossie's inspiration. He had based his softly feminine, flowing dresses on her shape, particularly when she was pregnant.

By this time Ossie was as well known as the pop stars he numbered among his friends. In 1970 Mick Jagger introduced him to Bianca and Ossie designed her dress for their wedding in St Tropez in 1971, although, on the day, she wore Saint Laurent, having not told Ossie that she was pregnant. With her big shoulders and small waist, she had the perfect figure for a new trousers phase, which began at this time. These were cut in a similar way to a man's trouser, fitting close on the hips with a tight waistband and turn-ups. Jean Shrimpton had one of these. 'I wore one of his trouser suits to New York, beautifully tailored, low cut at the front with a peplum.' Adie Hunter describes this as a very feminine, but butch look. Ossie made Bianca an all-in-one cream brocade suit with big shoulders and men's trousers, which tied at

David Hockney, Mr and Mrs
Clark and Percy, *1970–1.*
Acrylic on canvas.
Photo: Tate Britain. © David Hockney

right

Jean Shrimpton wears an Ossie black crêpe lounge suit, embroidered with strawberries and green leaves in a Celia design, curvy waistcoat bound with red and green satin piping, high-collared jacket with breast pockets, bound in satin and green ric-rac. Vogue, *August 1971.*

Clive Arrowsmith © Vogue/ The Condé Nast Publications Ltd

opposite

Auburn-haired Nicky Samuel wears the 'Tulip' dress, draped across a studio table covered in a crewel-work 17th-century tablecloth at her house in Mallord Street, built for Augustus John just before World War I. It was the location for an Ossie show in 1972. Vogue, *December 1972.*

Norman Parkinson Ltd/Fiona Cowan

the neck. And a wonderful camel wool coat.'

In 1972 David Hockney drew her wearing this coat, which was calf-length and puffed-shouldered with a yoke, tying at the waist in a pre-New Look 1940s style; she was also wearing suede sequin shoes by Manolo Blahnik. The image was featured in *Vogue*, along with his drawing of Celia wearing a shoulder ruffled, open-necked silk chiffon dress with her own print, dated November 1972. The drawings show an emphasis on the shoulder and full sleeves; they illustrate both his innate romanticism and his ability to produce streamlined, practical outerwear. [65] Bianca also wore his chiffons, however. He described

a dress that he made for her in 1971. 'The front panel is 44 inches of chiffon drawn in into four inches. No, that's not true. The shoulder and the front is the same piece of cloth, the sleeve going down and the front panel is the same piece. I am very proud of that dress, and it was directly through Kathleen's influence…I got her to draw out the threads to gauge on, which you couldn't get anyone to do now.' [66]

Hockney designed the invitation for a show, with a small audience of 100 people, that was held at Nicky Samuel's house at 28 Mallord Street on 20 November 1972. The small Chelsea townhouse had been built for the artist Augustus John and had one huge beautiful

Tulip dress in bias cut silk chiffon,
Celia Birtwell print, 1971.
© **Warrington Museum**
and Art Gallery

light room painted in shining dark red, which had been his studio. After several other owners, Christopher Gibbs had worked with her to return it to former glory. Knowing that it was to be the scene of a Quorum event, *Vogue*'s Catherine Tennant arranged for Norman Parkinson to photograph Nicky at the house, draped across a table covered in a crewel-work cloth, wearing a chiffon dress with a huge tulip print by Celia. The article appeared in the December issue of *Vogue*.[67] 'I had all the arrogance of youth,' she says. 'When he arrived I was still in my nightdress and asked him, "Have you photographed anyone I know?" He said, with great charm, "The Queen." "Anyone else I know?" I asked.'

Norman Bain recalls the event: 'It was quite intimate. That was the thing about Ossie; if he was asked to choose between a big A-list event or something more private, he would always choose the latter.' 'Ossie had models that were people in his life,' says Nicky Samuel. 'It was that thing of exclusivity and friendliness which other places, like Granny Takes a Trip, didn't

above left
Ossie's drawing of a jacket and pleated skirt, c. 1972.

above right
Ossie's drawing of a coat dress, 1972. The yoke and waist are very similar to the camel wool coat worn by Bianca Jagger in Hockney's drawing in Vogue, April 1973.

have.' Nevertheless, the audience numbered members of the Royal Ballet, including his friend Wayne Sleep. Bianca Jagger flew in from Jamaica to model alongside Patti Boyd, Kari-Ann, Gala and Carina Fitzalan-Howard. Suzy Menkes wrote: 'The models wore fitted bellboy jackets with pointed fronts and printed revers. Soft blouses were gathered at the waist, there were curvaceous jumpsuits and wispy chiffons. There were big tucked coats and prints on fine jersey. Everywhere there were big rounded shoulders and narrow waists. The effect was feminine, sexy and stunning…Wouldn't the ideal be for a benefactor to step forward, who would set up Ossie Clark in his own studio, and organize production on a streamlined basis with couture standards?' [68]

The fact that Suzy Menkes was asking this question when Ossie had a backer in place indicates that there were serious problems for Quorum. It was rumoured that Alice Pollock had ended her partnership with Ossie and her contract with Radley. The cause of this ruction was not specified, nor is it clear why she and

Ossie eventually went separate ways, but it was a disaster. Ossie asked John Kasmin, gallery owner and art dealer for David Hockney, to be his business manager. It was apparent that his business relationship with Radley was strained: on the one hand, Al Radley was desperately trying to get him to work; on the other, Ossie, who was capable of being extremely stubborn, was depressed by the reality of mass production in Britain. Being paid a salary and royalties had made him very well off, but it also meant that he was effectively employed by a company which simply did not have the kind of system or allow the creative freedom of a French counterpart, for all Al Radley's good intentions. Ossie saw himself as an artist and his materials were the most beautiful fabrics available. 'The idea of a diffusion range was quite new, but Radley took it to its simplest form,' says Adie Hunter. 'Al Radley found it very hard to deal with Ossie. Alice knew how to modify something that was extreme. Ossie found it difficult because he saw things being so watered down. He was copied so much anyway in

Dress and coat with butterfly print, one of Celia's early designs, c. 1967.

Black evening suit with sequinned tulip design on the jacket in red and green appliqué, c. 1973.
© Warrington Museum and Art Gallery

Britain and America that he wouldn't speak to the other designers brought in by Radley to Burnsall Street; Betty Jackson, Marie France, Sheridan Barnett. He went back to Radnor Walk, where he worked best.'

Nicky Samuel, who also bought couture from Yves Saint Laurent, argues: 'He was an artist, the best things that he did were like a work of art; they are timeless. Saint Laurent never had to think about anything except designing dresses. He could create what he wanted. At Saint Laurent you could get everything in one place, 20 shirts from the rail and haute couture. It was such a different set up from wonderful Ossie, where you'd hope that something would be made in three months by a couple of wonderful women who sewed for him. In those days in Britain, people didn't know where someone like Ossie should go. People were looking in the King's Road for fashion designers; Ossie was far more special. He knew he was good, but he couldn't sell himself.'

In 1973 recession set in, and the miners' strike was followed by the start of the three-day working week early in 1974. Biba was offering glamour on a less expensive and grander scale at its Kensington High Street store; designers Anthony Price, Bill Gibb and Zandra Rhodes were the rivals who increasingly challenged

Ossie as the press sought new stories and new stars, but everyone was badly affected by the new economic and social climate. Ossie, now part of an older generation, was increasingly in danger of appearing stuck in his 1960s past. Malcolm McLaren and Vivienne Westwood epitomized the new mood. They opened Let it Rock at Paradise Garage at 430 King's Road in 1971, an emporium for retro clothing and 1950s kitsch, and it was soon a magnet for Ossie's glamorous friends, art and design students and dyed-in-the-wool Teds. It was fresh and exciting, surrounded as it was by hippy emporia, and it was alternative to the too-established Quorum down at the smart end of the King's Road. [69]

Interestingly, for his collection of April 1973, he was influenced by 1950s glamour, not the 1950s that he could remember only too well from his working-class childhood, and which appealed to McLaren and Westwood. Again Alice arranged for Black Magic to sponsor a box of chocolates for every person. The cover of the box had a man in a 1950s-inspired suit with a trilby hat and a Rosalind Russell-style 1950s vamp wearing an off-the-shoulder Ossie dress with Celia print sleeves. 'Step out of an old-fashioned chocolate box or biscuit tin in one of Ossie Clark's sumptuous tarts' dresses. This chocolate-box vamp wears a skin-hugging all-revealing dress by Ossie Clark for Quorum £42...Her soft-centred companion wears a canelloni type of suit, an incredible suit, designed by Anthony Price for Stirling Cooper. Pale-grey worsted wool, it costs £28.' 'Michelle, the black model from Mendes, in a cloud of pinks, floating on mescaline. Alice – please can we wear it off the shoulder? Tony Howard did the music, Pattie Harrison twirling; Kellie, Gala,' he noted. [70]

In July he presented his autumn collection for Radley at the fashionable Aretusa restaurant in Chelsea, offering glamour to a public hit by recession. Joan Juliet Buck reported for *Women's Wear Daily* that 'Clark fans took over most of the show with waving, kissing and cheering. Bianca Jagger was there in her summer dress, summer hat and summer cane. Eric Boman was there with the initials E. I. embroidered on his shirt. "I haven't done the B yet." John Kasmin, Ossie's business associate, was there, sitting with Nicky Samuel and Amanda Lear. Ulla (Larson) of the antique market kept buys taking pictures – a new London pastime.' [71]

Black models paraded the collection. 'The clothes are a summer mixture of all that Ossie does best – pale crêpe dresses in baring shapes with Celia Birtwell's pineapple, and flowers printed all over them. He also puts a wrap skirt over a short romper suit. Evening looks come in black and gold, but the shape for both day and night is the same – relaxed with plunging necks. The lengths: long and short.' For *Drapery and Fashion Weekly*, Suzanne Turower praised the accessibility of the collection. '"Ossie's best yet," was the comment most heard as Ossie-wearers such as Bianca Jagger, Marianne Faithfull and Patti Boyd left after seeing how these brilliant designs can be translated into realistic "Radley" prices for volume selling to the trade.' [72]

In 1973, Ossie and Celia separated and in October 1974 they divorced. This event shook Ossie fundamentally, and although they continued to work together, he lost the one stable thing in his life that enabled him to find his creative way. His Autumn/Winter 1974 show was staged on 25 March at the King's Road theatre where *The Rocky Horror Show* was running.

Working on the collection, he wrote in his diary for 15 May: 'Making boned bodice and green lace – designing in my mind. Pattie 2 o'clock. Ravishing beauty – fitted bodice on her. She said how secure it made her feel.'[73] *Vogue*, reporting on the event, informed its readers that David Hockney, Marianne Faithfull, Linda and Paul McCartney were in attendance.[74] Also present were Britt Ekland, Ringo Starr, Bryan Ferry and Rod Stewart. The look was again long and aimed at eveningwear, but it was self-consciously glamorous, with a romanticism that was not in sympathy with contemporary fashion. Waists were nipped in and breasts pushed up and out by beautiful

'He created an incredible magic with the body and achieved what fashion should do – produce desire.' Manolo Blahnik

Victorian-style tightly boned bustiers; chiffon dresses with Celia prints floated less than in the past, off the shoulder with ruched and fitted bodices. It was too soon – this sculpting of the body was not to become acceptable until Thierry Mugler, Jean Paul Gaultier and Azzedine Alaia responded to the new body-conscious mood of the mid-1980s. Manolo Blahnik commented, 'He did a 19th-century bustier and made it Chelsea Girl. Time has not touched the things of Ossie yet.'

The 1975 show on 11 November in which Marie Helvin, Jerry Hall and Nicky Samuel modelled was again distinctly romantic in feel, but had lost the edge of the distinctive 'Ossie look': masterly cutting, breathtaking prints and always, a new idea. Possibly the ability to visualize an entire collection that would appeal to a younger audience had been lost, but the clothes he made for a particular woman still flattered her shape, were beautiful and made her so, too. 'The things he made for me in the later years are collection pieces,' says José Fonseca. An article in *The Sunday Times* by Michael Roberts was curiously spiteful; the voice of the new generation, he implied that Ossie's glory days were behind him. 'People fought to get into Ossie Clark's hour-long show, they did not all get in. Those who did saw very tall cataleptic models wearing frilled chiffon dresses. There was wild applause for a gauze cape with a Klu Klux Klan hood. Many loved the show, some hated it...Ossie tends to talk wistfully of the days when he and Hockney and Celia and friends held afternoon teas, did paintings of one another, exchanged bunches of tulips and called one another "petal". But now it's all over, and while Ossie designs through the night, the diary in his Chelsea studio remains completely blank.' [75]

Despite being put in the same category as his friend, Hockney, however, is aware of the differences between the world of fine art and the applied art of fashion. 'He worked in the rag trade but they didn't know how to deal with Ossie, it was simply a different period. Certainly, he had enormous natural talent and perhaps not enough discipline that normally you would think an artist can impose on themselves. When I was making the painting of Celia and Ossie, when he was doing his collection, he would work intensely for a few weeks before. When they were done and had the show he would then totally collapse and not do anything at all for a few months. I couldn't have done that. Probably he didn't know how to do that because of the nature of the way he worked.'

'There was no conception about how fabulous he was and it is an example of why British fashion always fails. He needed a good business partner to support him,' says Vanessa de Lisle. The following years saw a struggle that ended just as people in the British fashion industry were beginning to both re-evaluate and appreciate him. In a moment typical of the uncertainty he now felt about himself, he noted in his diary, following the publication of Georgina Howell's article in *The Sunday Times* which featured many images from the highpoints of his career, 'Amazing of Celia to say I am a genius and, what's more, that no one refutes it. Am I a genius? Certainly I've never thought so. Instinctive, extraordinary, imaginative, creative capacity.' [76]

Ossie, you were brilliant.

Acknowledgements

I would like to thank everyone who has helped with and worked on the book, especially Ossie's friends and admirers, including Marit Allen, Norman Bain, Patti Boyd, Stevie Buckley, Angela Childs, Kathleen Coleman, Tony Costelloe, Jenny Dearden, Vanessa Denza, Christopher Gibbs, Dr Susannah Handley, David Hockney, Georgina Howell, Adie Hunter, Sandra Kamen, Barry Lategan, Vanessa de Lisle, Candida Lycett Green, Beatrix Miller, Wendy Pearson, Leslie Poole, Fiona and Frances Ronaldson and Nicky Samuel. I am extremely grateful to Harriet Wilson at Condé Nast and the staff of the *Vogue* Library; Janine Button, Lisa Hodgkins, Simone Burnett and Brett Croft; and to Mary Butler and Monica Woods of V&A Publications, my editor Catherine Blake and to the curator of the Ossie Clark exhibition at the V&A, Sonnet Stanfill. Thanks also to Vaughan Oliver, Chris Bigg and Lee Widdows at v23 and David West at Studio 22 for the book's design; to Thomas Persson, Susan Howard and Mark Hughes for their help at the beginning of the project; and to Ulla Larson and Henrietta Rous, who first helped me to research Ossie Clark. Very special thanks go to Ruth Marshall-Johnson for her painstaking work and support. To Al Radley, who has worked so hard to get the exhibition staged and has believed in both the book and the show, but most of all, thanks go to Celia Birtwell, without whom none of this would have been possible.

Notes

Introduction

[1] *Cherry Gray was assisted by Celia Birtwell and Brian Harris.*

[2] *Linda Watson, 'Ossie Girls',* Evening Standard Magazine, *29 July 1994.*

Manchester: 'A very confident boy'

[3] *Ossie Clark, lecture to students at the Royal College of Art, recorded by Dr Susannah Handley, 1996.*

[4] *Ibid.*

[5] *Ibid.*

[6] *Ibid.*

[7] *Ibid.*

[8] *Ibid.*

[9] *Ibid.*

[10] *Candida Lycett Green, 'A Rare Bird',* British Vogue, *July 1999, p. 12.*

[11] *Ossie Clark, lecture, 1996.*

[12] *Barbara McGrath, 'Student Ann wins "busman's holiday"',* Evening Chronicle, *28 June 1961.*

[13] *'Fashion Show by Students',* Daily Telegraph, *28 June 1961.*

[14] Drapers' Record, *17 February 1962.*

Royal College of Art: Let the magic begin

[15] *Ossie Clark, lecture, 1996.*

[16] *Ibid.*

[17] *Janey Ironside,* Janey *(Michael Joseph, London), 1973.*

[18] *Ossie Clark, lecture, 1996.*

[19] *Ibid.*

[20] *Ossie Clark's obituary,* The Independent, *13 August 1996.*

[21] *Shirley Lowe,* Sunday Mirror, *10 October 1965.*

[22] *Ossie Clark, lecture, 1996.*

[23] *Ibid.*

[24] *Ibid.*

[25] *Ibid.*

[26] The Ossie Clark Diaries, *edited and introduced by Lady Henrietta Rous (Bloomsbury, London), 1999, p. xx.*

[27] *Ibid, p. lviii.*

[28] *Ibid.*

[29] Vogue, *August 1965.*

[30] *Shirley Lowe,* Sunday Mirror, *10 October 1965.*

'The Wizard of Ossie'

[31] *Magazine cutting, Alice Pollock, no title, no date, c. 1971–2.*

[32] The Sunday Times, *7 March 1971.*

[33] Vogue, *November 1966, p. 114.*

[34] Diaries, *p. lxi.*

[35] *Simon Kavanaugh, 'Ossie Clark, Britain's fashion king', cutting, no title.*

[36] *Georgina Howell, 'The Dressmaker',* Sunday Times Magazine, *12 July 1987, p. 28.*

[37] Diaries, *p. lxiv.*

[38] *Laver did not mention Ossie Clark in his* A Concise History of Costume, *but he recognized Ossie and Celia's influence, and the changes that they manifested in their work. 'It may be that the extreme shortness of the mini-skirt will be modified in the comparatively short future…Recently there has been what seems like a revival of femininity, with a definite Oriental flavour. This may point to a new development of fashion, some entirely new line, or it may be not more than a ripple on the stream, leaving its main direction undiverted and undisturbed. Only time can tell. The only certain thing, it seems, is that the desire to make oneself attractive to the opposite sex will always play a part in the clothes young people wear.'* A Concise History of Costume *(Thames and Hudson, London) 1969, p. 273.*

[39] *Ossie Clark, lecture, 1996.*

[40] Vogue, *no date.*

[41] Nova *interview, no specific date or page reference, 1967.*

[42] *Marit Allen,* Vogue, *March 1968, p. 123.*

[43] *Nadeanne Walker, 'A Blatantly Nude Look From London Designers',* International Herald Tribune, *7 August 1968.*

[44] Vogue, *15 October 1968, p. 75.*

[45] The Times, *no date.*

'The King of the King's Road'

[46] *Felicity Green, 'The Importance of Being Ossie',* Daily Mirror, *9 June 1969.*

[47] *'Spotlight',* Vogue, *June 1970, p. 134.*

[48] *'Double Take',* Vogue, *November 1970, p. 116. The working title was 'When I die I want to go to Vogue'.*

[49] *Alice Pollock, cutting, no title, c. 1971–2.*

[50] *Ossie Clark, lecture, 1996.*

[51] *'Is it Goodbye Chelsea, Hello to Paris?',* Evening Standard, *8 March 1971.*

[52] *Quoted by Deirdre McSharry, 'Ossie and his Womanly Women', cutting, no title, no date.*

[53] *Ossie Clark, lecture, 1996.*

[54] The Sunday Times, *7 March 1971.*

[55] *Quoted by Deirdre McSharry, 'Ossie and his Womanly Women', cutting, no title, no date.*

[56] *Ibid.*

[57] *Alison Adburgham, 'A lucky thing happened on the way to the Quorum,'* Guardian, *13 July 1971.*

[58] *Marit Allen, 'News from Paris,'* Vogue, *June 1971, p. 4.*

[59] *Suzy Menkes, 'Ossie Reveals All…',* Evening Standard, *26 May 1971.*

[60] *Judith Watt, 'Design Classics',* Evening Standard Magazine, *26 November 1999, p. 43.*

[61] *Ibid.*

[62] *In fact, for the Spring/Summer 1972 collection, Blahnik, untrained but brilliant, made shoes with high heels of rubber but without a solid core to take the weight of a body. Under the hot lights on the runway, the rubber began to soften. The shoes, however, looked stupendous and no-one in the audience noticed.*

[63] *'Is it Goodbye Chelsea, Hello to Paris?',* Evening Standard, *8 March 1971.*

[64] *Ibid.*

[65] *'Ossie Clark Originals,'* Vogue, *April 1973, p. 82.*

[66] *Ossie Clark, lecture, 1996.*

[67] *'Precious Original',* Vogue, *December 1972, p. 129.*

[68] *Suzy Menkes, 'On the significance of tonight's show, minus Alice,'* Evening Standard, *20 November 1972.*

[69] *Jane Mulvagh,* Vivienne Westwood, An Unfashionable Life *(Harper Collins, London), 1998, p. 54.*

[70] Diaries, *1999, p. lxxiv.*

[71] *Joan Juliet Buck,* Women's Wear Daily, *20 July 1973.*

[72] *Suzanne Turower, 'The Ossie Clark look – at down-to-earth prices,'* Drapery and Fashion Weekly, *20 July 1973.*

[73] Diaries, *15 March, p. 8.*

[74] Vogue, *1974, p. 23.*

[75] *Michael Roberts, 'Look! Fashion,'* The Sunday Times, *16 November 1975, p. 43.*

[76] Diaries, *16 July 1987, p. 221.*

Index

Page numbers in italic refer to the illustration captions on those pages.